There's Always Room At The Top

To order additional copies, please contact us.
BookSurge, LLC
www.booksurge.com
1-866-308-6235
orders@booksurge.com

ALAN S. BECKER

THERE'S ALWAYS ROOM AT THE TOP
The 8 Secrets of the Super-Successful

2006

There's Always Room At The Top

TABLE OF CONTENTS

CHAPTER 1
INTRODUCTION TO SUCCESS

Who does not want success? We all want it!

Can we all achieve success? Of course, we can. For different people success may mean different things, but however it is defined it is within reach.

Can you come directly out of college and succeed without investing twenty years of painful trial and error? Yes, you can.

Can you achieve success without a college education? Yes, you can.

Can you turn around your life and career in your thirties or forties or fifties and find success for the first time? Yes, you can.

There are secrets to success that the people who have reached the top in their fields and the people who enjoy the most accomplished and fulfilled lives have found and apply every day. They are not great, unsolvable mysteries accessible only to the privileged few. They are available to each of us, and the purpose of this book is to share the secrets I have discovered and provide practical advice that will open up doors for you and give you the tools to "make it."

If you are thinking about success, you have already taken the first step toward getting there. Merely making the choice to pick up and begin reading this book shows that you have the interest and motivation that are essential in the quest for a successful life and career

This book is intended to give some practical guidance on the rules that will make it easier to achieve success. Some of the secrets we all learned when we were very young, as children in a playground. Think of the concept of the "Brass Ring." Younger people are at least vaguely aware of the Brass Ring as having to do with winning a prize. It is probably only when you are lucky enough (considering the alternative) to be over 50, that you are likely to know the derivation. Nevertheless, the phrase endures.

I remember the Brass Ring quite well from my youthful days at the park. We would go to Coney Island to enjoy the 10 cent hot dogs (!), salt air and the rides. Every Merry-Go-Round (or, depending on where you are from and when you were born, the carousel) had different shaped seats on which the young people would sit. The best seats were on the outside perimeter (usually the seating was three deep); and the best of the outside seats were the horses that went up and down on the pole to which they were attached, as the carousel went 'round and 'round.

At one location around the circumference was a mechanical arm, and at the tip of the arm was a brass ring. Usually the Brass Ring was just out of reach for most people. As the carousel went around, those sitting on the outside seats (and if the seat was a horse that moved up and down, the most advantageous timing was as the horse was coming up) would reach out for the Brass Ring each time they passed by. You would really have to stretch. This combination of good timing and stretching beyond your normal reach, along with a little bit of luck, resulted in the occasional child (no one appreciated an adult going for the ring—it was not quite the same challenge) snaring the ring. It could then be turned in to the operator for a prize. Merry-Go-Rounds are still around, but the Brass Rings are gone. Undoubtedly they would no longer pass muster with the safety regulators. An unsecured child, reaching for the brass ring, stretching beyond his or her normal reach on a rapidly rotating mass of moving parts, would entail a high degree of risk. It was a risk that we all happily undertook, but older, wiser heads apparently determined was not in our best interest. One of my partners pointed out to me that the risk was real and probably more than few youngsters reached beyond their capability and landed on their heads. That may be true, but assuming no permanent damage, the ones who were destined for success undoubtedly got up and tried again.

In a very real sense, the Brass Ring is a metaphor for Life. In order to win Life's prizes, it requires good timing, it requires that we stretch, and it requires that we be willing to take risks. (A little bit of luck also helps, but **frequently we are able to make our own luck.**) Not everyone will snare the prize, but it is possible for everyone to feel the exhilaration of going for the Brass Ring.

These days many people come out of school, high school, college, and even graduate school, with a lot of substantive knowledge, but virtually no guidance on how to achieve success in life (and career) once having attained that knowledge. I believe the fundamentals of success can also be learned, and that you cannot start too soon to acquire the knowledge and habits that lead to lifelong success.

This book will provide you with those fundamentals, both from my own experience and the experience of many of the most successful people in the world in their various fields, who I personally interviewed for this book. In this first chapter, I will provide the outline of what is to come: (1) Success stories of Great Americans; (2) The Fundamentals of Success; (3) The Eight Secrets of the Super-Successful. First, I will introduce those highly successful people I interviewed, and use life lessons derived from them in the subsequent chapters. Chapter 2 will be important in that it will attempt to define success, since it is hard to find something if you cannot define or describe it. In Chapter 3 we will hear from the highly successful people about some of their defining experiences. All of us have experiences in life which define us. In the pursuit of success, some of us are aided by those defining moments or experiences, and some of us must overcome them. They largely form who we are, but they do not determine if we can or will be successful; only the degree of difficulty or the path to take. Chapters 4 through 11 will describe the Eight Secrets of Success.

The secrets or rules you will read in this book all grew out of my personal experiences—experiences in politics, in business, in life. I had not read any of the books in the field at the time I first compiled my "secrets for success." Only later did I begin to read books on management, marketing, leadership, and success. (I had been a psychology major in college, so I had already done a lot of reading on psychology and behavior.) When I did start reading these books, I began to see the patterns and realized that some of my own rules were time tested, expressed differently by people who had lived similarly and understood achievement.

I remember the day I first put together my list of the things I had learned about success. It was 13 years ago. I had just taken my older daughter to her first day at college and was helping her get set up in her dorm room. It is a dangerous thing to offer a teenage daughter advice on life, but I decided to take the risk. "Do you have paper and a pen handy," I asked. She did. I said to her, "I am going to give you a short list of things I would like you to remember. If you learn these ideas and live by them, you will be assured of success in life." I proceeded to dictate 10 points (I have since combined a couple), offering a short explanation for each. To my pleased amazement, she wrote them down and listened. The chapter headings of this book are essentially those points first articulated that day in a very hot dorm room. I think both my daughters have done well using these principles, as have others I have shared them with over the years. I think they will serve you well, too.

Great American Success Stories

Most of the big life lessons come through experiencing. Nothing I can tell you will be as lasting a lesson as that you learn for yourself, by going through an experience. In fact, if it is a negative experience, you will probably take away more from it than you would if things had gone just right. Living it is the best way of learning it.

However, when it comes to success, it does not hurt, and it often helps, to draw on the experience of those who have traveled the path before you. If nothing else, learning how others have seen and grasped opportunity, have overcome adversity, have persevered through difficulty, have maintained a positive outlook in the face of negative events, can be a source of inspiration and strength.

For that reason I decided to interview a number of great Americans who have reached the very top of their chosen careers—be it politics, sports and entertainment, business. What is more, all have done it with style and all have had success which has stood the test of time. In the succeeding chapters, I will excerpt quotes from the interviews to put with each chapter where relevant. (I correctly anticipated that their advice, drawn from their experiences in life, would support the various points I made.)

Well into doing the interviews, I noticed an interesting coincidence (except, I don't really believe in coincidences. There is usually more to it than that.):

Except for the two elected political leaders (each of whom was second or third generation elected public official), **all** of these hugely successful people were either first generation Americans, or, if not, were the first generation in their family to attend college. Perhaps, therein lies the subject of another book. I won't try to analyze it here, except to say that perhaps it lies in a greater hunger to achieve, or a greater belief in the opportunities afforded by our land of opportunity, unspoiled by being too comfortable or too practical. Whatever the reason for this phenomenon, I thought it worth mentioning.

Obviously there are many more successful people than these few. In fact, I myself probably know hundreds of highly successful people, by anyone's standard. In all likelihood, you do too. But, I selected these because they are all high profile. You either know their names already, or you know the company they run, or the organization for which they are known. You will also see a heavy bias in favor of people from Florida. It is not that Floridians are more successful than other people; merely that, as someone who has lived his entire adult life in Florida, these are the people I know and had ready access to. The important thing, though, is the lessons to be learned from their stories. Those are universal.

In the subsequent chapters I will refer to these people by name when I quote from them, but let me introduce them to you here. The men and women I interviewed for this book are:

Madeleine Albright. *Madeleine Albright was born in Prague, Czechoslovakia. Her family moved to England as Hitler rose to power, and later to the United States. She went to college and later earned her Ph.D. She held a position as Chief Legislative Aide to U.S. Senator Edmond Muskie and then was a member of the National Security staff. In 1982 she became a Professor at the Georgetown School of Foreign Service. In 1992 she was appointed by President Clinton as Ambassador to the United Nations, and four years later as U.S. Secretary of State, serving until 2001. She now heads* The Albright Group, *an international consulting firm.*

Governor Jeb Bush. *When Jeb Bush arrived in Florida, he helped start a real estate company that today is one of the largest commercial real estate companies in Florida. In 1987-88 he served as Florida's Secretary of Commerce. Following an unsuccessful bid in 1994 for the Governor's Office, Gov. Bush founded the Foundation for Florida's Future, a not-for-profit organization to influence public policy, and co-founded Florida's first charter school. He was elected Governor in 1998 and re-elected to a second four year term in 2002, becoming the first Republican to be re-elected Governor in the State's history.*

Jorge de Cespedes. *Jorge de Cespedes came to the U.S. with his brother Carlos as children in the early 1960's as part of the secret Operation Peter Pan program, which sent 14,000 children to the U.S. Today,* Hispanic Magazine *lists them among the 10 wealthiest Hispanics in the U.S. After college, Jorge and his brother became pharmaceutical sales representatives and later started their own company, PharMed, which has become one of the leading distributors of medical, surgical and pharmaceutical supplies. He also is a part owner (with*

Bob Johnson, founder of BET) of the Charlotte Bobcats of the NBA. In 2003 he was named Ernst & Young Entrepreneur of the Year. Jorge is known for his philanthropy as a major contributor of time and money to several South Florida colleges and universities.

Senator Bob Graham. *Bob Graham was first elected to the Florida House of Representatives in 1966 at the age of 29, and then to the Florida State Senate in 1970. A member of a wealthy dairy and real estate development family, Sen. Graham was elected Governor of Florida, serving two terms until 1986. In 1986 he ran for the U.S. Senate and upset an incumbent Senator. He was easily re-elected to two more six year terms and served until January 2005, when he retired. In the critical post 9/11 period, he served as Chair of the Senate Intelligence Committee, and in 2004 authored a book,* Intelligence Matters.

Wayne Huizenga. *H. Wayne Huizenga left college and after a stint in the U.S. Army started a small garbage collection company with one truck. That company became Waste Management, Inc., the largest such company in the world. He then started Blockbuster video stores.*[1] *After selling Blockbuster, Wayne started AutoNation with one site and that now has grown to be the largest auto dealership (with over 370 dealerships) in the country. Another public company formed by Wayne is Extended Stay America, which has over 500 hotels around the U.S. Wayne also was the first owner of Major League Baseball's Florida Marlins, the NHL's Florida Panthers and is the owner of the Miami Dolphins of the National Football League. Wayne and his wife are generous philanthropists in Florida. In 2004 he was named Ernst & Young's Entrepreneur of the Year.*

Brad Meltzer. *Brad Meltzer was raised in Brooklyn and Miami. He graduated from Columbia University Law School.* The Tenth Justice *was his first published novel and became an instant New York Times bestseller. That was followed by four more bestsellers. His books have over six million copies in print. Brad is also co-creator of the TV series* Jack & Bobby *on the WB Network. He has been featured on the Today Show and in major publications like Time Magazine and USA Today.*

Clarence Otis. *Clarence Otis grew up in the Watts section of Los Angeles. He began his career as a Wall Street attorney, and then an investment banker. He became Treasurer of Darden Restaurants, Inc. (owner of Red Lobster, Olive Garden, and Smokey Bones restaurants), and over the next decade worked his way up to Chief Financial Officer, CEO of the Smokey Bones subsidiary, and then President and Chief Executive Officer of Darden. He is one of just 18 African American CEOs at America's 1000 largest pubic companies, and was listed by*

Black Enterprise Magazine *as one of the 75 most powerful black executives in corporate America.*

Susan Story. *Susan Story received an engineering degree from Auburn University and her MBA from University of Alabama. She went right to work for the Southern Company in 1982 and rose though the corporate ranks, becoming President and CEO of Gulf Power Corp (a Southern Company subsidiary) in 2003. She is the only woman CEO of an investor owned electric utility company in the United States. In addition, she was selected as 2005-2006 Vice-Chairman of Enterprise Florida, the public-private economic development agency for the State (the Governor is always Chairman, but the meetings are run by the Vice Chair, the private sector leader).*

Nina Tassler. *Nina Tassler graduated from Boston University planning to be an actor. After trying New York, she and her husband, TV actor and director Jerry Levine, moved to Los Angeles where Nina became a theatrical agent. Soon she changed career track again, going to the production side of the entertainment business and moved up the ranks at CBS to be head of drama development. In that role she was responsible for bringing to the screen many of CBS's top rated programs from* Judging Amy *to* CSI. *In August, 2004, she was named President of CBS Entertainment. She is responsible for overseeing all Network programming for prime time, late night and daytime, as well as program development for all series.*

If you enjoy meeting these enormously successful people, and enjoy their stories and life lessons half as much as I enjoyed doing the interviews, I guaranty you will come away from the experience enriched with inspiration and wisdom.

Fundamentals of Success

I am reminded of a call from my younger daughter when she was a junior at college in Boston. She was visiting a friend in New York City. The friend's father is one of the best motion picture directors of our era, respected by those in his field, recognized and admired by most of the American public. My daughter called to tell me of something surprising she had learned. She said to me, "You're one of the most successful people I know, and my friend's father is certainly among the most successful people in the country, at the top of his field. My friend and I were comparing notes about our parents and I thought it was interesting that both of our fathers—for all they have accomplished—still listen to tapes and read books about success and self improvement."

While it might seem odd that people who have (at least by the estimate of others) achieved a great deal of success still seek to learn more about the subject, I assure you it is not all that odd. Sammy Sosa is probably among the greatest baseball hitters of our time, yet he still takes batting practice. Tiger Woods is undoubtedly the greatest golfer of this generation, but he will still go out every day and hit hundreds of practice balls. Both men still have coaches and still listen to their advice. The reason for this seemingly superfluous attention to the basics, is that these men, as with all successful people, recognize that however great their achievements it is important to **always be aware of the fundamentals**. A commercial airline pilot, even if he has been flying for twenty years, begins each flight with a review of a written checklist. When the stakes are high, you do not take chances or risk sloppiness. It is critical to **learn and maintain good habits**, and there is always the risk that we will backslide into bad habits.

Similarly, success is a habit. There are fundamentals (which will be discussed in this book) that are common to achievement of success, and habits to be learned which will promote success. Those good habits should be continuously reinforced.

Susan Story, CEO, Gulf Power Co.:

One of the great things about Michael Jordan, of course, when he was younger in his career, it did look like he could fly. He would fly across the court, but what most people don't know is, as he got older, he realized he couldn't jump quite as high, he couldn't do some of the things he did physically. Do you know, before practice, before the Bulls would practice, he would go to the gym 2 hours early and he continued to practice his lay ups, his fundamentals, his basic ball handling skills. **This is a man who was the top in his field, who would go early before the other folks and continue to work on his fundamentals because he thought, as I am growing in my career, there are some things I don't do like I used to but I need to make sure that I'm developing skills to help me continue to be at the top of my game. And those are based on the fundamentals that I always learned.** *I may do those fundamentals a little differently, but I'd better know how I can maximize them or optimize them now.*

I think that's the best example of us as leaders continuing to hone those basic skills, like honesty, confidence, forward looking, inspiring. Those are four basic characteristics, but, a one time shot 5 years ago does not make those the same today. How I express integrity? The competence I have changes daily with the burgeoning technologies we've got out there. The forward looking. For me to be able to set a direction for my company and for the people that work here, I've got to know what's happening in the world. What's happening internationally—how's it going to affect the business? How's it going to affect our communities. And then inspiring, once I've helped set a vision, set the target, how can I get people on board? How can we speak to people's hearts, because their hands and their minds follow their hearts.

It is never too early or late in life to **learn the fundamentals of success**. If you learn them before you enter college, you will certainly achieve more in college, both academically and in otherwise getting the most out of the experience. If you learn them in college, that too will enhance your college career and give you a major head start as you leave the hallowed halls and enter the "real world". And if you had not mastered the knowledge and habits that lead to success in college, it is still not too late. With any luck at all, "after college" lasts for a very long time.

Sometimes you learn lessons in your student years that don't have their full impact or achieve their full meaning until much later on. I remember an incident that occurred when I was 17 and a freshman in college. I had come to Miami Beach, Florida for spring break and stayed at a small ocean front hotel. The hotel was owned by an old lady by the name of Mrs. Evans. She owned a vast amount of real estate, but anyone looking at her could never guess from the way she dressed that she could put together the cost of her next meal. For some reason Mrs. Evans took a liking to me, and she decided to share with me some of her wisdom and business advice. And, for some reason, even with the ocean at our doorstep and a lot of things to do in Miami in April, I enjoyed hanging around and listening to her stories and her advice.

She gave me three basic rules to become wealthy, which I will share (please do not take this necessarily as an endorsement, merely a recounting):

1. Buy and hold real estate. But buy it just beyond where the development has occurred and wait for the development to come to you.

2. Go to the race track every day and bet on the favorite horse to "show" in every race.

    (A "show" bet is a bet to come in third place in the race, and you will get a payment—lower than if you bet on a horse to come in first—if the horse comes in first, second or third.) If you do this for the whole season, you will never make a killing but you will get a ten percent annual return on your investment, which is not bad.

3. This one she pointed at me for emphasis, and solemnly said: "Remember, No partners!"

I can only wonder where I would be today if I had taken all of this advice. (Actually, I did not do badly buying real estate, but never to the full extent of her recommendation.) Success has its rules and Mrs. Evans's rules certainly worked for her.

Put aside excuses that delay your quest for success

I know some readers will ask, *"But before I learn to achieve success, don't I first have to find myself?"* The answer is, "No." **Finding yourself has been highly overrated.** The "self" is not a place where one ends up. You will not "find yourself" hiding in a closet or behind a wall. Finding oneself is a process, and it does not end. **When you stop learning and growing you start dying.** If anything, the mere practice of the success attitudes and techniques taught in this book will aide in the process. The very acts of "doing" will result in insights to who you are and where you are going, and hence facilitate the "becoming." It is a journey, and it begins now. And you might as well enjoy the journey. As 19th Century poet Ralph Waldo Emerson wrote, "Life is a succession of lessons which must be lived to be understood."

I am also aware that with some of the recommendations I make, your first reaction might be, "Sure, but that is easier said than done." Of course it is. Everything is easier said than done (although we all know blabber mouths whose sole apparent object is in the saying...of anything). Certainly anything worthwhile is easier said than done. But again, it starts with the desire, then requires the discipline and effort, and with repetition becomes habit. **With desire, effort and repetition, you will have transformed the difficult to the possible,** if not the easy.

REFLECTIONS AND APPLICATION—CHAPTER 1

At the conclusion of each chapter I am going to include exercises to help focus your attention and efforts on the subject of success addressed in that chapter. It will include questions for you to ask of yourself and action steps for you to take. I call them these "Reflections and Application" because I think it more accurately describes what I am asking you to do. It is important that you become an active participant in your success. You cannot achieve the levels you want to reach merely by being a passive reader. So, let's get you engaged in the process.

1. What does "success" mean to you?
2. If success includes material wealth, how much annual income would you deem necessary next year to consider yourself successful? How about in 5 years?
3. What single thing is most important to achieve in your life?
4. Are you willing to make significant changes in your life to reach this goal?
5. Who is the most successful person you know <u>personally</u>? (It might be a family member, family friend, neighbor, teacher, etc)
6. Why do you consider him or her as successful?
7. This week, call that person. Ask her (or him, but being politically correct and constantly writing "him or her" really bogs down the writing, so I will use them interchangeably) if she will spend a half hour with you to discuss how she became successful. Set a specific date and time to meet. Be prepared with several questions about her goals, how she set them, how she achieved them. If you have a goal of your own, ask for advice on how you might achieve yours. If the person has been free with her time and advice, ask for permission to call her occasionally to share your progress and ask for further advice. Most people will gladly agree to this. Then be sure you do so. If you know a second successful person, repeat the process. Within a short time you will have an invaluable network of "mentors."

CHAPTER 2
DEFINING SUCCESS

Before going into any discussion of the strategies and tactics to achieve success, it would be helpful to define, what is success? In all likelihood, different people will see success differently. For some it is money. Others see success in terms of achieving power. Still others find it in fame—being recognized. There are people who are deemed successful by virtue of their service to the community. Many people see success in the pleasure of a loving family. In truth, it is probably any or all of these things, as *your* definition will determine whether you can or will achieve success. It is also a definition that can, for you, evolve as you experience more of life and more of success. As with most things in life, there must be balance.

Madeleine Albright, former Secretary of State:

> *Well, I think that the time that I really felt truly successful, was when I first got named to the United Nations, because my hope had been actually to be involved in public policy. I loved being a Professor and I think, before that, in terms of my professional life, I considered just getting my Ph.D. a big success, because it took me a very long time to get it. But the fact that I was finally able to combine my interest in politics with my interest in foreign policy at a time in my life working for a President I really liked, that seemed like the greatest thing. And then, of course, then I became Secretary; it was kind of over the top. I never believed it would happen and when it did, it was just a sense of having arrived. Of course, it was just the beginning of four very interesting years, which I loved every minute of them.*

I asked her if doing something she really enjoyed was a big part of being successful. She replied,

> *I think that is a very good question. For me, it is. I think that **you can't really think you're successful if you're in something that***

doesn't make you happy. Because no matter what the job, if it's drudgery, or you feel that you're in the wrong job, then you may be judged successful in somebody's eyes, but in your own eyes it is hard to say that is success. You asked how I measure success—I think that the best way to measure success is to try to think that you have made a difference in a field or in a avocation that you really like and if you feel that you've made a difference in it, or even if you're not working, if you have hobbies or something, I think if you feel that you've made a difference in something you like, I think that's success.

Jeb Bush, Governor of Florida:

My definition of success has kind of evolved over the years. When I was younger, much younger, I would say success was accumulating wealth. The pursuit of that for some reason gave me a sense that I would be successful if I made money because I would be providing for my family. I got married really young and I had three kids, all of whom are adults thank goodness, but when I was young it was really related to making money. It seems so important to provide for your family, but it doesn't seem like that's a very good measurement of success anymore. And I don't measure it in victories because in my world right now it's very transactional. I got a series of things, you know a list of things to do that is about 8 pages long. I keep it in my computer and there's lots of wins and loses and so winning isn't the measurement of success anymore either, although I am very competitive and I like to win. When I win it doesn't add value to my life. I guess now in my life it's giving back, is the measurement of success. Having the ability to give back and sustain it over a long period of time and do it in a way that doesn't necessarily draw attention to yourself. It's an evolutionary thing, it changes as your life changes.

Jorge de Cespedes, President of PharMed:

[My definition of success] changes I guess. What success was to me in my 30s is a little bit different than what success was in my 40s to now I am developing what success is in the 50s. I'm 51 years old now. In my 30s, success was clearly all about money. I would have identified success as how much money can I make at that time and I'm going to be judged against other people: what kind of car

do I drive, where is my house and etc. etc. **As I turned 40 success was more about accomplishing goals, about being successful within the industry, about leaving a legacy where that industry could make a little bit of difference.** *Something that my name would be associated with. A big improvement. My particular interest was health care distribution.* **And now in my 50s I think I find success is not so much what you've done with yourself, but what you want for other people and helping other people become successful, enjoy wealth.** *I really get off on that now a days.*

I suggested to him that it was interesting that as wealth became less of a measure of success, the more wealth he accumulated, and he said, *Absolutely. It's a phenomenon. Not only that, but the less you want people to know that you have that wealth. In my 30s it was very important to me that the people I grew up with knew that I was doing well and that I drove a van, I lived in a big house. Frankly now, at 51, I kind of shy away from that.*

Bob Graham, former Governor of and U.S. Senator from Florida:

That [definition of success] *is a very good question. Sometime ago I was on a rich man's yacht and by the front console of the yacht there was a sign that said "the one who wins is the one with the most toys". The yacht, I guess, being a manifestation of that. I don't agree with that definition of life.* **I think life is, the success of life is judged by your own sense of personal gratification. It's judged by the influence that you have on others.** *I think if there is one single test of how well you've lived your life it is how well your children turn out. Throughout your years on this earth you can fool a lot of people, put on a mask and make believe you are something that you are not. You can't do that with your own flesh and blood, living intimately with you. They are going to pick up the real essence of your values and so if you want to know how successful a person is, ask what kind of kids did he or she raised.*

I observed that by that measure Senator Graham has done pretty well. He agreed:

I'm very pleased; we have 4 daughters. We have 11 grandchildren. We are extremely blessed.

Wayne Huizenga, billionaire entrepreneur, owner of the Miami Dolphins:

Well, when I first started in business in Fort Lauderdale, my goal was to be a large company in our industry just in my market and it wasn't until we went public and had the currency, meaning the stock, not cash but we used our stock as the acquisition tool and went around the United States, and the first time in my life really thought, "hey we could build a big business, and not only in the United States." We went out of the United States and so from that point on I never really looked at things on a local level anymore. I always looked at them on a global level.

Since that time in the early days we look at, we kind of really focus on the big picture rather than the small. Everything we do today, even though we have lots of companies today that are private, people don't know about them.... Of course, now as I get older, I do more things based on what my kids want to do. Something that I would have done, maybe they don't want to do, so there's no sense in me doing it at my age. So I'm really trying to help them get set up in their businesses. We made a family decision based on my friends that I've seen. A lot of my friends have a family company and when the father retires or passes away, then 1 or 2 of the kids end up staying in the business and 3 or 4 of kids are not in the business, and usually that leads to disruption in the family. Some of the business, flying around in the corporate plane, running the whole thing, you know it's not the same. I first noticed that in Joe Robbie when I bought the football team from Joe Robbie and he had 9 kids at that time....The family fought and I said then, you know I'm not going to let that happen to my family . So what we're doing now is we buy businesses and each child, I have 4 kids, and each one has their own business. Some have bigger goals than others. Some are happy to have 3 or 4 small things and others want to do more, but when my time comes where I'm not working anymore or I pass on, then each one of my kids will have their own business and I don't have to worry about my kids feuding with each other down the road.

Brad Meltzer, novelist:

*In my opinion, **I think that success is always self-defined, and I think you're only happy with your success if you are a happy person to begin with. Someone once said to me that miserable people can live anywhere and they'll be miserable and happy*** *people can live anywhere and they will be happy. I think similarly that applies to success as well. In my opinion, success has nothing to do with money or fame or any of that nonsense. I think success is the answer to the question—are you allowed and able to do what you love to do? And if the answer is yes, then you are very successful and anything else just becomes something that gets caught up in, probably the trap that we in society put on ourselves. But to answer your question about whether I feel I'm successful, I'm just happy. I feel like I'm lucky and fortunate to be able to do what I do and that people pay me to talk to my imaginary friends and on that alone I can't ask for anything more than that.*

Clarence Otis, CEO, Darden Restaurants:

*Well I think **success is really sort of realizing your dreams, whatever those might be, and you define success for yourself.** I learned earlier about my parents in their 20s, how they and all their friends, in the context in which they were living, were really high achievers. I mean because they had the drive and the ambition to want to go some place where they could do more than they had and that same desire for achievement. That probably defines success.*

Susan Story, CEO, Gulf Power Co.:

*That's an interesting question. I think, actually through my career **when I think about success, I think, "am I happy with my life and what I'm doing?" It's not necessarily gauged by how much money I have made or what people consider to be power, but am I making a difference?** As I started my career, of course growing up the way I did in a rural Alabama town, I didn't know what a president of a company was or a CEO of a company was. I started as an engineer in a nuclear power plant and just believed in working as hard as I could and doing the best job I could because that's the way I had been raised. I started progressing pretty rapidly through managerial ranks and, interestingly, never really looked at what the next job would be.... I just kind of kept progressing through the ranks. When people would say, "why are you successful," I guess my bottom line answer would be just that **I enjoy I everything I do, I put everything I've got into it, and I want to be part of the team that does great things.***

Nina Tassler, President, CBS Entertainment, Inc.:

> *I think it's a combination of a number of things. One,* ***it is a sense of confidence, a sense of accomplishment, a sense of creative freedom.*** *Being at a position in my life where ideas that I have, thoughts that I have, I'm able to put into effect, share with other people, as well as listen to other people's ideas and implement them.* ***I think it's also about being at a stage in life where you have a sense of freedom, sense of maturity, a sense of—a very optimistic view of life in general.*** *There is the obvious, which is the financial freedom, but I think for me personally most significantly it's the creative freedom. There are certain parameters and certain boundaries, but I'm very comfortable living within those.*

You can see from these very successful people how the definitions of success may vary, and how they evolve over the course of one's professional life. In every case, while all have had financial success, money plays a relatively minor role compared to factors like family, independence, freedom, creativity, and the general enjoyment of life.

I personally know several billionaires and several more centi-millionaires (which I guess proves great wealth doesn't rub off). Among them I know some that have strong family bonds, give back to the community (often unheralded), enjoy their money but also put it to good use. I know others who continue the ruthless pursuit to accumulate more, more, more (often simply as a way of "keeping score"), and whose families have been touched by divorce, disease, death, and even suicide. The outside world seeing the enormous wealth of these individuals might consider each to be "successful", but on closer examination those lives tell a different story. Success is clearly much more than achieving material wealth (not to take anything away from financial security). Who is successful? In many ways, success, like happiness, is not a mantle that can truly be placed on someone until he has fully lived his life. I once heard an old saying (my mother tells me it is from the ancient Greek philosopher, SoLon): "count no man happy until he has died." The same is true of success. We don't know the full story until life has been lived to the end. But there surely are indicia of success.

Do I consider myself successful? Only in a very limited way. I have seen psychological studies of successful men and women which conclude that many very successful people feel a little guilty because they do not believe they are nearly as successful or accomplished as other people see them. This has been called the "imposter syndrome." For this reason it is probably better to withhold personal judgment. I will concede, though, that most people consider me successful. They can see the obvious facts: I was elected to the Florida Legislature at an early age and served three terms; I was responsible for the introduction and passage of important consumer and environmental legislation; I moved to Florida as a student, with no contacts or family there, and within a relatively short time started a law firm which has become one of the top 15 in the state. They see that I am well known in the community, that I am Consul General for the Czech Republic, and I am on several statewide and community boards. I have accumulated a fair amount of real estate and with it some material well being. More importantly, I have two wonderful daughters with whom I can actually talk about virtually anything, a beautiful young grandson, and a wife who is a loving partner and friend. True, stuff can happen, but for now this is certainly success enough for me.

It is easy to look at those who have achieved great wealth and count them successful. I can give a good example, though, of success through *sacrifice* of money. In 1990 one of my law partners, Jeff Streitfeld, announced to us that he wanted to give up practicing law and seek a judgeship. "But Jeffrey," I said, "You realize that if you do this you will no longer be able to afford the big house you live in or the Porsche you now drive." I still recall his answer: "I know, but I will still be able to live in a house better than I grew up in." To Jeff, far more important than the money he was making or would in the future make, was the respect and prestige of being a judge, and the ability to make decisions that would have an impact on people's lives.

Most important, he wanted the ability to spend more time with his family. Today, Jeff remains a judge who gives unselfishly of his time and who is always ranked among the top judges in our community for his intelligence, fairness and sound judgment. Just before he was about to assume office, Jeff said to me: "you think I'm crazy, don't you?"

"No," I replied. "I think you are very courageous and unselfish, and if you ever read that I won the Florida lottery look for me to follow your lead."

The important point is that success can be learned and should be learned early. There are many books on the subject, many experts from whom to learn. Not surprisingly, it is not magic. If you study successful people, such as those interviewed for this book, or in the literature of success, you will find themes repeated over and over again. Often they are expressed differently, use different examples, are called something else—but the fundamentals remain the same.

For example, Warren Buffet, the second richest man in the world, repeatedly expresses the virtue of compounding (think compounding interest) when building wealth. Two of the leading motivational gurus of our time are Tony Robbins and Brian Tracy. They apply the same concept to self improvement. Robbins talks of the power of compounding; Tracy refers to it as the law of accumulation. They are talking about the same thing.

Just as money grows through compounding, so does success at accomplishing changes you want to make in yourself. If, for example, you suddenly decided you wanted to lose 20 pounds and tried to do it all at once, you would fail (or the achievement would only be temporary). If you determined to eat a little better and exercise a little more and lose 1/4 of a pound every day, in less than 3 months you would have lost the 20 pounds and done so in a way that did not disrupt your life, but rather made for habits that insure more lasting change. If you are running a C average and want to get it up to A, it would pose an overwhelming challenge to move to A the immediately following semester. Better to improve incrementally and go for B next semester and A after that (either way, it is surprising how slowly the grade point average creeps up). If you wanted to be a better salesman and increase your sales by 50%, the increase would seem daunting and would appear like a mountain too steep to climb. If, instead, you determined that each day you would be 1/10 of 1% better, at the end of one year you will have improved by 25%. The impulse to do it all at once is probably the reason no one keeps their New Years resolutions. **Think baby steps. The virtue is in those little increments that, over time, make for big change.**

Finding Happiness is Essential to Finding Success

As you may have picked up from my discussion of success this far, achieving wealth or fame without personal happiness, cannot result in a truly successful life. Having a lot of money but being miserable most of the time is not something to which any sane person aspires. Like success, happiness has its rules. They are more appropriately found in the writings of others devoted to the subject. (One of my favorites is *Happiness is a Serious Problem* by Dennis Prager.) Still, there are some pretty basic ideas that can set the stage for a happy life, and thereby prepare you to reach, and as important, appreciate a life of success.

Happiness, like success, is susceptible to different definitions and interpretations. What is happiness? Most people are acutely aware when they are unhappy. Happiness is more elusive. There was a time I might have concluded that "I am not unhappy, therefore I am happy." But having been "not unhappy" all of my life, I came to realize that it is much more than that. It is seeing, finding, feeling the joy of life. It is looking forward to a good night's sleep after a fulfilling day, and looking forward to a great day when you first wake up in the morning. It does not mean that you are never ill, never sad, never disappointed, never struggling. Yet it relates to **an inner calm and feeling of well being, the ability to appreciate the good in yourself and in others**, and a preference for that good. While it is quite possible to find material wealth, recognition and stature without being happy, by my definition, it is not possible to be truly successful without accompanying happiness.

There have been stressful days when I have looked out of my office window at the fellow sitting on a mower cutting the grass, alongside the shimmering lake in our office park, under the beautiful blue sky and warm Florida sun. "There," I thought, "is the life! The man has no worries (other than whether it might rain) and gets to enjoy the fresh air and beauty of nature."

But in truth, we know better than that. We cannot say whether any other man is happy since we are not aware of his family situation, of his unfulfilled dreams, of physical or mental pains he endures. Haven't we all known people that "have it all" and yet are not happy? Haven't we known people who, by virtue of bad luck, injury or illness, loss of a loved one, financial disaster, have every right to be unhappy but who, instead, choose to be thankful for what they have and look forward to the future with hope? It is in such encounters that we find clues to the essence of happiness. **Those who are grateful for what they have and eschew resentment for what they do not have are far more likely to be happy.** Those who **choose a life of optimism over one of pessimism** are much more destined for a life of happiness and achievement.

How bad or good an event or a condition is, to a very large extent, depends upon how we choose to look at it. Our personal experiences help shape the meaning of happiness for each of us, and our choice of how we look upon life is frequently the determining factor in our happiness. In short, happiness is a choice.

Susan Story, CEO, Gulf Power Co.:

- *The **happiest people are not the ones that have had the easier lives**. Have you ever noticed that? The people that are given everything, that things are "easy" for, they're not the happiest people you find. **It's not what happens to us. It's what we do about what happens to us that determines our happiness, our joy and our success, in my opinion.***

Close to 35 years ago I read some books by the well known child psychologist, Dr. Haim Ginot. Although I had been a psychology major in college, I read these towards the end of law school, for no particular reason other than that I had heard him interviewed and it seemed that he had an interesting approach. In his works I found some insights that are useful in attaining both happiness and success. Dr. Ginot discussed the reaction of parents whose child engages in flights of fancy. If little Johnny says, "I saw a giant," the reaction of too many parents would be, "no, Johnny, there are no giants." A far better reaction would be, "ok, Johnny, you saw a giant. Why don't you tell me about him?" Dr. Ginot explained that as a parent you are not *agreeing* with Johnny that he saw the giant; you are merely *accepting*. Acceptance of how other people feel will endear us to them to a far greater extent than disagreeing openly or agreeing disingenuously; hence, a lesson for success. Yet, acceptance—of what is, of how people are, of conditions outside your control—makes it far more likely that you can be happy. And being happy makes it far more likely that you can be successful.

In counseling acceptance, it is important to distinguish what is within your control and what is not. If you are unhappy with your physical fitness, you certainly could accept it as it is. You would therefore be less likely to be unhappy about it (putting aside the concerns about future health and the ability to engage in a range of activities that the lack of fitness might preclude). But it is a condition you can do something about, and taking control is an alternative (and in my view, preferable) path to happiness, since in most cases you have control over your level of fitness if you choose to assert it. Similarly, if you did not pass a test for advancement and have the opportunity to take it again, you can accept that you are too stupid to pass (there really are some people so negative that they would rather think the worst of themselves than put in the effort to change it), or you can accept that this time you did not do all you could but next time you will study harder and make sure you do what it takes to pass. And don't worry about it too much anyhow. Some of the smartest people in the world do poorly on standardized tests. It is well worth the time and effort to worry (in the sense of expending mental energy, not developing anxiety) about things that are in your control, things you can change.

It is not worth the expenditure of energy to worry about those things you cannot change. There was an accident and someone died. You have a disease that requires constant medication. You lost a job that you loved and which paid good money and there is no other such position anywhere. All might be good reasons to go through the stages of grieving first recognized by the late Dr. Elizabeth Kuebler-Ross. These include denial, anger and depression. But remember that the final stage of grief is acceptance. Then you move on, and **deal with those issues that are within your control.**

The attitudes of happiness and success

I find that in all walks of life there are so many people who whine about their past or their present lot, who see the glass half empty instead of half full, who always see the obstacles and ignore the opportunities. Such people are annoying and I try to avoid them. Negativity is contagious, like many other diseases, and I prefer to be **around positive, "can do" people who take responsibility for their lives.** Such people are far more likely to be happy, far more likely to find success, and you are more likely to be happy and successful if these are the people you are around.

A couple of years ago I read *The Art of Happiness* by the Dali Lama and Dr. Howard Cutler. After reading it I called my mother and told her I had not realized my father was a Buddhist monk. My father, now in his 88th year, never went past the eighth grade. He started his own retail business and was good at it, enabling him to retire when he was 52. He never worked after that, although my mother started college in her 40's, went on for her Masters degree and taught school until she retired at 75. My father says the deal was that he would work the first half of their life together and she would work the second half….and that is how it turned out. Now they spend their days taking long walks, doing exercise, reading, talking with friends and family. My dad takes no medications whatsoever—if he really gets sick, maybe "a Bufferin". My mom took nothing until she turned 80 (I hope she will forgive me for revealing she has passed that milestone), and now only a couple of preventative medications that have been prescribed. My father is the type of person people talk to. Not just "hello." Friends and even strangers seem to tell him their life stories and pour out their woes. He dispenses advice and people listen. My whole life this has been the case, and generally my father's advice has been sound as a guidepost for those in search of happiness. His wisdom comes from a place somewhere within…not from anything learned in school or read in a book. Thus, my conclusion, that he is the reincarnation of a Buddhist monk.

Even as a young child I remember some of the lessons I learned from my father. He would always tell us to hate no one. "Hate does not hurt the person you hate, but it hurts you." This is so true. He cautioned us not only that we should not speak ill of others, but that even if someone else was knocking a person we knew, that we should never agree. "Some people like to cause problems," he warned. "If you agree with Ellen that Mary is selfish, then the next person she discusses it with she will say 'Lorraine thinks that Mary is selfish' and that will find its way back to Mary. Better to just listen and say nothing." Boy, that one has saved me a lot of trouble over the years.

The most enduring and emphatic lesson in my father's repertoire is "You must **love yourself and take good care of yourself** if you would have the ability to love others." The same message comes from the Dali Lama, and I know for a fact that my father was telling us this even before the Dali Lama was deposed from Tibet in the 1950s. It is so simple, yet so fundamental to leading a healthy and happy life. Never listen to anyone who tells you (explicitly or, more likely, implicitly) that you are not worthy of your own love or anyone else's. Avoid such people like the poison they are.

Just a short while ago I heard the Dali Lama speak in person at a University gathering in South Florida. He told about his recent illness. He had had a lung infection and a bad cough. He went to Delhi and the doctors diagnosed the infection. They gave him medication and in a couple of weeks it had cleared up. Said the Dali Lama: "They think it is their medicine. I say it is half their medicine and half my attitude." This is the message of my father, and one I have found over and over in life to be true: **our mental state can have a material impact on our physical health and well being.** Think healthy. (Likewise, you can learn to think wealthy, think happy, and think unselfishly—the conditions, more often than can be explained by coincidence, follow the thought.) Tell yourself over and over again that you are feeling better and will soon be well, and it will aide in recovery. Tell yourself that you are sick and getting sicker—and sicker you will most likely be.

At the same appearance the Dali Lama described the nature of a contented (happy?) individual. He said that he, like any man, sometimes felt negative emotions such as anger or jealousy. Fortunately, he said, these **negative emotions are like waves at the surface of the ocean: they come and go, but beneath the surface the ocean is always calm.** Therein, so simply expressed, is what I consider the essence of happiness. People often remark that, even under the most difficult circumstances or faced with apparent provocation, I always seem calm. It is true, and I can assure you it is a choice. I am told that it can often be extremely annoying to my loved ones who would like to see occasional emotion. Of course they mistake lack of angst for lack of concern, lack of demonstrative excitement for lack of passion. It does mean you have to go a bit out of your way to let your loved ones know how you truly feel, since an unintended by product of your security can be insecurity in others.

You can **choose inner calm.** Couple that with caring for others, a positive outlook, acceptance of what "is" and the determination to take action to change what "can be," and you are well on your way to the happiness that must be the underpinning of any truly successful life. **People who hold on to their anger, their fears, their jealousies, cannot be happy and are actually deterred in their pursuit of success.**

The aspects of happiness are also valuable as instruments of success. We have all heard the old expression, "it is better to give than to receive." That may or may not be true, but I can assure you that willingness to share, a readiness to give to others—be it assistance when they are in need, something tangible, a thoughtful gift, comes back multifold to you.[2]

It is also possible to give too much, and this was another lesson I learned from my father. Early in my career I had a partner who had grown up in different circumstances from mine. He had grown up poor and deprived of a father's love. I had always known love and abundance. When it was time to open an office together, he could not afford his share, so I was willing to provide the entire investment. My father cautioned me that I should not do so much. He said it was commendable that I wanted to share in that way, but that human nature was such that the person to whom you gave so much would end up resenting you because he had to take it.[3] I ignored the advice from my father, which later proved to be prophetic. When I later began a second partnership in the practice of law, this time I did not put up the money. We each signed equally on a bank note (which was paid off within the first year—I do not like debt). That partnership has survived over 34 years and counting.[4] So, with giving as with so many things, it is a matter of balance. In most circumstances, **it is more rewarding to be generous.**

Generosity can be expressed by the giving of tangible things, but also by the giving of love and attention. I have never actually thought of the projection of love and caring to be a strategy for achieving success. Yet, I have seen that it often works out that way. I remember my very first case in the private practice of law. I was representing a lady police officer who had been unfairly deprived of her pension benefits. I had a good case but the judge on the case was a very old man, very tied into the establishment. He had his old friends who could get quick access to the courtroom and very little apparent regard for young lawyers for whom he never made time. In fact, it was nearly impossible to get hearing time with him or to get a ruling after a hearing. Access to him was difficult because he had a long time secretary who was cold and tough and intimidating. I decided that access to the judge was going to be through the secretary, and the way I would do that would be to show her that, unlike most lawyers in town, I was not intimidated. I determined that each time I was in her presence I would smile and send out vibes of liking, even loving her. I would mentally project "I like you, I love you, I love you, you are a good person" whenever I approached her desk. In almost no time at all, she began to smile (something never seen before by the members of the Miami Bar) and I had ready access to the judge for hearings. And, although he was slow to rule, somehow the rulings on our case seemed to come more quickly. And we won. I realized then how important state of mind can be, and how contagious. You can **project positive feelings out to others and they will reflect back to you.** And by all means, be nice to the secretaries.

Madeleine Albright, former Secretary of State:

*The thing that I found is, **you never know who is going to help you along the way and people that you meet, not that you should be looking at people as to how can this person help me or not, but the people that you meet often under one circumstance end up being very helpful to you in another. Mostly this is advice, that it pays to be polite and nice to people.** Somebody that you're rude to under some circumstance may end up being very important to you, and so, I had a lot of stories about how one thing lead to another, but Zbig Brzensky was my Professor at Columbia. He then gave me the world's great job when I worked in the Carter administration.*

Wayne Huizenga, billionaire entrepreneur, founder of Waste Management, Inc., Blockbuster Videos, AutoNation and owner of the Miami Dolphins:

*When you are in business you want to think about what you can do to give back, and you want to think about what people are going to think about you when you're not around anymore; and the type of legacy you are going to leave. And **you want to always be known as someone that's fair and square and treated people with courtesy and respect; and somebody that if they gave you a hand shake, that their word was good.** That's the most important thing, to be able to have the people feel that, "hey, I can deal with that person, I can trust them and I can feel confident if I do business with them that I'm not going to get stepped on". That, I think, is the biggest thing that we talk about and through the years, **we've had lot of chances in life to take shortcuts and we've always focused on: we don't take shortcuts, you do it the right way, you make it happen properly, you treat everybody with respect. I've tried to instill that into my kids.** You only go one way: you do it first class and you do it right and you treat everybody with courtesy and respect no matter who they are, how much money they have or how*

*much money they don't have. Treat everybody the same and you know
in life you will be remembered not as a person who has a lot of money
but you will be remembered in life as a person who treated everybody
with respect, and a genuine nice person.*

Giving begets getting. If you give of yourself, be it your time or
your money, to others who are in need, you will experience a feeling of
well-being that is hard to explain or describe. It feels good to be able to
help others—not for the recognition or the thanks, but simply for having
the ability and will to do so. That alone would be sufficient reason to be
generous of spirit. Yet, I have also discovered that if you **unselfishly help
others to achieve their goals**, they will invariably go out of their way
to help you achieve yours.

Jorge de Cespedes, President, PharMed:

*I grew up hoping to be…I thought that I could be a baseball player.
I'm a pretty descent baseball player, all City player, South Florida.
I guess like many young men, dreamed of being in the big leagues. In
reality, as a kid, maybe I was a little too fat, a little bit too slow—
that wasn't going to happen. I started coaching, and I've always had
a love for sports and to this day we run the Company in a very much
sports orientated way. You could describe me not a President of the
Company, more as the head coach, and **I do what any good head
coaches do, which is go out and find great position coaches.** You
know you could correlate to the head of finance would be your offensive
coordinator, etc, etc. We kind of have that mentality and once we hire
an assistant coach to learn the particular part of the team, we pretty
much let them dictate how they want to run that part of the team, and
we have been very, very successful with that. The other mind set that
we have here at PharMed which is unlike many other companies, and
certainly not too many that I have been associated with, is that we live,
eat and sleep, that nobody works for the department. People work <u>with</u>
the department. That's a mindset that once you get people to buy off on
it and they really believe it, and I think, we really have it going here.
Our people realize, you don't work for Jorge or Carlos or PharMed.
You work <u>with</u> Jorge and Carlos and PharMed. Once they buy that in
their minds, you've really got it going. They take an ownership of the*

Company without really owning any of it, and they're really pushing forward.

So, I said to Jorge, a big part of achieving your goals is helping other people achieve theirs.

Absolutely and you know, as I mentioned earlier, certainly the last four or five years of my life, I'm thrilled every time I see you know one of our employees buying a house or have the opportunity to buy a Mercedes. This past year in 2004, we had 9 people become millionaires. They own stock in the Company and there was a refinancing. They had the opportunity to sell their stock back in January of 2004, 9 millionaires. Nine people became millionaires here at PharMed. To me, I was thrilled and it was a tremendous proud moment when I got to pass out those checks.

Susan Story, CEO, Gulf Power Co. told me that by helping others achieve their best, it brings a whole lot more back into her life.

*I've found as I've moved up into executive ranks, it really is true, **that the more you give credit to others, the more you look good and you don't even have to bring it on yourself. I think those who truly try to help others, build others up and help them look good, are the people that the best people want to work for.** And that's what I found in this organization. One of the best compliments is—is working for Susan, is that a place that I will get recognized, rewarded and promoted from? And that's the type of reputation you set up. That she can help me to develop to my fullest potential, and I will get credit for what I do. And so…to me, my success is based on the success of the people I work with every day….*

*I will tell you—**of all the things I enjoy about my job, probably the best is helping people develop to their fullest potential.** There are people who come up and, Alan, some people really don't know what they are capable of doing. When you push, it's not always easy, when you push and stretch people, you get a lot of push back, sometimes at the beginning. Some people don't make it, but for the most part, those who come through are bigger, stronger, better than they ever thought before. That, to me, is one of joys of my job. It's to see people actually reach that. The person who is my personal mentor is a man named Charles McCreary. He is the current President and CEO of Alabama Power, which is a sister company of ours within Southern Company….*

He would push me to do more than I ever thought I was capable of doing. He would be there if I needed him, but never telling me how or what do to. Here's the bottom line: go out and do it, and I knew he was there, as a safety net, but I didn't need him to be there all the time. That's the kind of leader I try to be, which is, I'm going to give you the bottom line, but I'm not going to tell you how to do it, and I want you to become the best person you can be. I think 99% of the people want to work in an organization for a person that helps them develop to their fullest potential. And the organization always benefits from that.

Nina Tassler, President, CBS Entertainment:

*I realize that whenever anybody walks in my office, they are walking in for a reason and that they have something to say or they have something that they need and taking the time to listen to them and looking deeper into perhaps what the subtext is or whether something else is going on...**Management is not just about moving pieces around on a chess board, but it's also really being receptive to people's needs and problems and making them feel empowered and making them feel successful. I think you can measure the success you have by the level of success that the people have around you.***

A few years ago, a stock broker with whom I had a slight social relationship and no business relationship, asked me: "Do you know X (the Chairman of a major public company)?"

No, I did not know him. "Well, I know him and you two have a lot in common. You should meet him. Maybe he can become a client, but even if not, he is someone you should know." He set up a breakfast meeting for us to meet and attended himself to make the introduction. (P.S. the public company did later become a client.) He then repeated this with another introduction to another prominent business person in our community. Never did he suggest that there was anything in it for him or that he wanted anything other than to help two friends by introducing them to each other. A year or so later, our firm was considering changing financial advisors for our pension plan. As is often the case, several potential vendors were equally qualified. Who do you think got preference? Obviously, all other things being equal (i.e., quality of service and cost), I chose to give it to the firm of the stockbroker who had gone out of his way to help me and my firm.

Give first, with no expectation of getting in return and almost without exception you will be pleased to find, if not immediately then one day when you least expect it, you will get in return. It is not the reason to give, but it is a beneficial side effect. Oddly enough, when help is freely and generously given to you, the giver will usually be there to give still more. I learned this as a young legislator from an older, experienced friend, George Onett, who was a prominent lobbyist for what most people would call "special interests". It was perhaps the best advice I had ever received up until that time because it is so counterintuitive. He said that there were plenty of people who had information I would need or the ability to help me move ahead. Ask them for favors, he said, because "when you ask someone for a favor and they do it for you, they become indebted to you." Think about that for a minute. On the surface, it makes absolutely no sense at all. The reasoning behind it was this: once someone helps you (with advice or with a favor) they are invested in you and want to see you succeed. I have applied this time and again, and am continually amazed by its effectiveness. So, **ask and you shall receive**.

In another example of how **your own state of mind can affect your ability to succeed**, a number of years ago I evidently had too long a vacation, because I found myself thinking about what made some of our lawyers so successful (as measured in client loyalty, high fee collections, low accounts receivables, good results) compared to others. My thought was that if I could find the common denominator I could hire with that in mind, and perhaps train lawyers better to get more high achievers in our law firm. I spent a lot of time analyzing the issue. I decided it was not "hard work". All of the successful lawyers did work hard, but there were others, not as successful, who worked at least as hard. It was not "intelligence". While all were intelligent and had good academic backgrounds, there were many more who were at least as intelligent or well schooled and did not have comparable success. Then I realized the one common denominator: **the most successful lawyers were the ones who really cared about the clients** (and projected that caring). How do I bottle that? It is the little things, like calling on the weekend or night, with a thought about the client's situation; always returning phone calls the same day; calling occasionally just because you are interested and not billing the time. There is a lot to be said for doing something you like to do for people you like. Can success really be that easy? To a large extent, yes, it can.

Brad Meltzer, novelist:

> *Again I think it's all very much what you push yourself on. And I think it's all internal. If you're a miserable person, you've never going to be happy. Like these people who live in New York and just want to have all the money in the world and they are in a place where there is always going to be someone who has more than you, and if that's the race you're running, you've never going to win this race. I just refuse to run that race. I mean if I were running that race, I would put out a book a year, and I would put them out as quick as I could, and I would collect a check as quick as I can, and I'd try and race everyone to the top of that money pile. I just have no desire to do that. I write a book barely every two years. I take my time, I write what I love. I want it to be the best book it can be, and I want each book to be better than the one before. The only thing that scares me is, and we've all read these writers…When you read a writer and you read their book and you say, oh man, they're just phoning it in now. They've given up; now they are just, they're done…. {B}ut you know that's the only thing I care about. People put their money and their energy into these books when they buy them and they read them and I want them, when they close that book, to say that was the best book I read and that was worth every dollar I paid for it. I take that trust that a reader puts in me very seriously. So that's the only thing I care about. As long as I can put out the quality and I try to put out something good, I'm happy.*

Happiness starts with **giving yourself permission to be happy.** You deserve happiness, and anyone who tells you differently is either stupid or malevolent and someone to be avoided. Anyone who tells you that you do not have what it takes to be a success or that you do not deserve success or happiness is not a friend. There really are people who feel better about themselves by tearing other people down. Get away from them as fast as you can run in the opposite direction. **Believe in yourself.** Believe that there is good in life and in people and you will begin to see the good. In your personal life and in your business life, treat others as you would want them to treat you and you will be far along the path to success and happiness. I don't know where the Golden Rule got started (actually, try the Old Testament, Book of Levidicus, Chapter 19, and commentary by Hillel and Maimonides), but it has been around a lot longer than any of us or any of our books. Think about it. Live it.

CHAPTER 2 REFLECTIONS AND APPLICATIONS

1. Do you consider yourself a happy person?
    (a) If yes, what are the top 3 reasons—be they outside forces or characteristics found within yourself?
    (b) If no, what do you believe are the major negative conditions or missing factors?
    (c) What are the major causes of stress in your life?
    (d) Which of these are within your power to change or control?
    (e) With respect to those that you can control, list at least one positive step you can and will take this week to change or eliminate it.
    (f) List 3 things (events, possessions or people) in your life for which you are grateful.
    (g) Is there someone in your life who is negative and whose negativity brings you down?
    (h) If so, how can you avoid that person and the negative energy associated with him or her? (Or if you can't avoid them, how can you influence their lives toward more positivity?)
    (i) Are you often sick? What, other than medication, can you commit to do to conquer illness and remain healthy? (Hint: diet, exercise, avoid sick people, dietary supplements, think healthy....)
    (j) Are you angry or jealous of anyone? How do these emotions hurt you?
    (k) What is the first step you can take to "let it go"?
    (l) List 3 people who you will help achieve their goals. What are the goals and how will you help?
    (m) List 3 people who can help you achieve your goals (be it by means of an introduction, advice, etc.). Commit to take action this week (a phone call or visit to a-s-k).

CHAPTER 3
DEFINING EXPERIENCES WHICH AFFECT SUCCESS

A lot has been said about the role of nature in our success or lack of success in life. Certainly, there are genetic influences. Some people are simply smarter than others or stronger than others. Some are more predisposed to be caring, and some more genetically inclined to be cautious. However, I think the evidence is abundant that people with great natural advantages often fail, and people without those advantages—in fact, some with major natural impediments—often succeed.

A far better case can be made for the moments and experiences which shape our lives and our attitudes. These include the influences of our parents and our circumstances, as well as other factors so numerous as to be difficult to catalogue. I have always believed that success or not success starts with the individual's desire to achieve, then her belief in her ability to do so, and then in her willingness to take the steps necessary. Of course some people have an easier time of it than others. Of course some people are handicapped by life circumstances or setbacks. The latter group simply has to want it more or work at it harder, but success is just as much within reach. Sometimes, the very existence of adversity and obstacles aide in the drive for, and achievement of, success.

Many of the highly successful people I interviewed told fascinating stories of influences in their lives. I thought it worthwhile to share some of them.

Life Altering Events

Most of us grow up in a typically American household. We go to school, play with the kids in the neighborhood, watch TV, go to the movies. Pretty much the family life depicted on the American sitcom. Every now and then people experience events when they are young that leave a lasting mark, shaping who they are. Such formative events can be traumatic or uplifting. It is not so much the experience that matters as how the person reacts to it.

Madeleine Albright, Former Secretary of State:

> *Well, I came from a family where my father had been a Diplomat and so I kind of grew up, I had gone through many ups and downs in my life as my parents had. They had come from fairly well to do and put together families, and then had been refugees in England during the war, and then my father was an Ambassador and I was the daughter, and then we came here and had nothing again. And so my parents were the ones that really were able to teach us all about the fact that it was certainly nice to have material things, but that that was not was important. What was important was family. So we came here and I spoke English, very English English; my mother had a very strong accent; my father spoke English and my brother and sister were younger. And so it was really a matter of trying to fit in, that in many ways has been the story of my life, of trying to fit in. And so my first desires were to fit in to America and to just be very glad that we were out from under, in my case, the potential horror of living under communism.*

I asked **Jeb Bush** about his first race for Governor, in 1994, a race which he narrowly lost. I wondered how he bounced back four years later to win the 1998 Governor's race, and how the earlier loss had affected him.

Jeb Bush, Governor of Florida:

> *That's a great question. In fact I think **the greatest lessons I've learned in my life have not been the successes but the defeats.** The '94 experience was an awesome one for me because we, I started really with a lot of people having preconceived notions about me. They weren't necessarily...I had to work hard to earn people's respect because of the fact that I was the son of a President running for Governor not having worked my way up as you said. So I learned a lot on that experience and loss was very hurtful. I didn't immediately make up my mind that I was going to run. It took 2 solid years, but I took the time to stop...It didn't take long for me to realize that blaming others or blaming dirty campaigns...whatever, all the things that people around*

*me were saying, it didn't take me long to realize that that really was
irrelevant. That I should use this as an opportunity to be better as a
person.*

I suggested that basically he had to accept what he couldn't change and
move on, and he replied,

*That's right and take the opportunity to grow as a person, which I
did. I went back to work and back to business, but I also had my faith
which strengthened. I vowed to be a stronger, better husband, better
Dad. I gained humility, it's a great way to get humility losing an
election.*

*It's a good experience and so I don't think about this too much now. I
think if I had been fortunate enough to get elected in '94 I don't think
I would have been nearly as good a Governor as having gone through
the experience and lost, and done some soul searching about who I was
as a man.*

**Jorge de Cespedes, President of PharMed, part owner Charlotte
Bobcats,** is my next door neighbor. He shared an experience that could
make a wonderful movie, except for him it was not fiction:

*October 26, 1960 my father took my brother Carlos and me and my
brother Freddy on the plane. Eventually Freddy would be taken off
that plane and Carlos and I came up to Miami. We were told that
we were going to the United States for a few weeks or a couple months
maximum to learn English. My Dad didn't think that Cuba was
quite right and he wanted us out of there at that point and we were fine
with that. We would learn English and maybe return shortly. Well,
we got here and we would not see our parents again for a little bit over
5 years. We later got to be known, a very well known project in South
Florida called Pedro Pan or Peter Pan Project with a lot of kids. It
was the largest exodus of children in the history of the World. 14,028
kids in a period of 10 months were basically snuck out of Cuba, on an
airplane; can't get passports; no visa, no anything.*

*It was a combination of the American Government and Catholic
Church and the program called for children to arrive here in South
Florida. We processed for two, three weeks and then at the same time,
at Catholic masses all over the Country, parish priests were giving*

speeches about this situation and asking families to take some of these children. I believed my parents that they were only going to be a couple months, so even at the young age of 8, I knew that in the United States one had a lot of rights and I kept telling my social worker that, no, I didn't want to get assigned because my parents were coming. So I stayed, we stayed in the holding grounds for nearly 5 years. Two different holdings grounds. First we were in Florida City, Florida, which was the holding grounds for all the girls who had come to the Program and boys up to the time they turn 12. Then after 12, you were transferred, to Opa-Locka. So I stayed with my brother Carlos, who today continues to be my best friend and my partner. And we just adjusted. You just adjusted to life. I stared my entrepreneurial…I guess my first business success at the orphanage or the camp. We used to get a $1.40 every week just for our own expenses, to buy a soda, to buy a pencil, to buy a comic book, whatever. But in order to get that $1.40 you had to write a letter home to your parents. I saw an opportunity there. As Fridays would roll around, most of the boys didn't have their letters ready but yet wanted to get the $1.40. So during the course of the week I would write 4, 5, 6, 7, 8 generic letters, "Hi Mom, Hi Dad, I'm doing OK, weather is fine, food is good". You know, "I miss you, or I wish you were here" type of letters, and I would sell them. I would sell them on Fridays for $.25 each, and I had a pretty good customer base to a point where I myself wasn't having time to do what 8, 9 year old boys do, which is play and do whatever it is we like doing. So I knew we had the older girls in camp. I learned about the wholesale business that way. I got them to write letters I paid them $.10 a letter, and we sold them for a quarter. By the way I haven't made those kind of margins since—150% margins. I haven't made those since, but bottom line, 5 years later when my parents got here, I had saved $1,500.

Amazing enough, but there is more to Jorge's story:

I told you I would share a story. There's a lot in your life that prepares you for tough times. You hear the Wall Street people always talk about how they'd rather invest in a company that had a hiccup and come out of it than ones that never had a hiccup, because you never know how people are going to react when they have that first hiccup. Being brought up the way we were, you know, we had hiccups, many hiccups early in our life.

I remember we got here in October, like I said October 26 so our first Christmas was in December. We had an uncle, who was a doctor, who was doing ok and was able to get a lot of money out of Cuba and he invited me to his Christmas party. I was 8 years old. Picture yourself back then. There was a bus that would leave the orphanage and take you to Downtown Miami and from there relatives would pick you up. A relative had to write a letter that they were taking responsibility for you. So I quickly learned that was a way of getting out of there. So anyway, I got to his house on the 24th of December, which for Hispanics was even a bigger day then the 25th. There is a family meal and at midnight the gifts are passed out. Even at 8 I already knew Santa Claus didn't exist. Somehow I figured that out already at 8, but on that night it was, one of the key nights of my life because I think I became a man that night. There were many children, I remember the house being very close to the Orange Bowl so I was there and I partook and ate and so forth. When midnight rolled around all these kids were being passed out toys. I looked and I said to myself, wow, I'm sure there is going to be something there for me. Well, time came and went and all the toys had been passed out and there was nothing for me. I guess a relative realized when it happened and went to my uncle and said "listen, you know the kid didn't get anything," so they went ahead and put a dollar in an envelope, one dollar in an envelope and gave it to me. At 8 I was man enough at that point where I told them, while I really appreciate you asking me here, I don't need this and I gave the dollar back. I proceeded to leave the house, which would really create my first income opportunity here in the US. I didn't want to stay with him for the weekend. I knew the Orange Bowl was close by, so I walked over to the Orange Bowl, slept there that night. The following morning I hooked up with a vendor who sold sodas there at the Orange Bowl, and I would be his assistant. He'd pay me $5.00 a game for me to get cokes ready for him, and this and that. So for months and months and months after that when there would be games at the Orange Bowl, I would get one of the older girls to fake a letter like it was from my uncle so I could get on the bus for Downtown. And for months and months I slept in the Orange Bowl on Friday nights and Saturday nights to work there. Those things kind of make you grow up before your own time and felt about hiccups in life. There's not too much that happens *here at PharMed…we've had many many challenges throughout the years.*

A childhood experience like Jorge's would have to leave a mark. He explained the impact it had on him:

You know I pretty much went almost all through my 40s in denial of that [experience], that it had an effect on me emotionally. Being at Peter Pan is kind of like going to war. You depend on yourself and you depend of very very few other people. In my case, really the only other person than myself that I depended on was my brother Carlos and you grow up that way. It's hard to trust anybody else. It's hard, so you put a strain on a relationship with your family members, specifically your spouse. It's hard to let them into your life.

Have you been able to get better at that? I asked.

Yeah, I've worked, I've put a lot of time and energy, it's like anything else you do where you have to put in the time and energy to get through it.…part of your life.

Wayne Huizenga, billionaire businessman. Before Blockbuster, before the Miami Dolphins, before all the other businesses and sports teams, there was Waste Management which grew to be the largest waste disposal company in the world. Wayne told of the events that got it started:

My whole life has been a series of wonderful coincidences *or being in the right place at the right time, and that's how I got started. When I got out of the army and came home, my father took me to lunch and as we walked into the restaurant, which was the Yankee Clipper, we went to sit at a table and a voice rang out, said Harry, Harry, how are you? And my father turned around and it was a friend that he went to high school with. The fella was in from Chicago, his name was Herman Molder. Herman was down to hire a new manager for his small garbage company, which was based in Pompano Beach and so we sat down, we had lunch together, and they talked about the good old days and finally Herman turned to me and said, "what are you doing Wayne?" I said, nothing, I got out of the Army yesterday. He said good, you're my new manager. And I said manager, manager of what?*

He said, well I've got 3 garbage trucks in Pompano, the guy quit and I need somebody to run it, and I said no, no, I don't want to manage a garbage business, that isn't what I want to do. And he said ok, ok, just do me a favor, he said, just do it for 3 weeks so I can get someone. I can get someone from Chicago to come down and be the manager. Just do it for 3 weeks. Well the next morning at 4:00 I'm driving to Pompano Beach. Three trucks were parked at a gas station and so I did that for 2 weeks, 3 weeks, 4 weeks, 6 weeks, 8 weeks. I kept calling Herman, saying Herman when's this guy coming down here, and he said well, give it another month, and so I did it for a while, and maybe up to like 3 months or so. And so after about 3 months I was looking at a newspaper one day and there was an ad for a trash route for sale in Fort Lauderdale. Now back in those days the difference between Fort Lauderdale and Pompano was significant. There was a 2 lane road with a bunch of mangos on it going to Pompano, and so it was 2 separate cities. I talked to the fella that owned this trash route and he had $500 a month worth of business in an old beat up truck. So I cut a deal with this fella to buy his business. He ended up financing me for the $5,000. Gave him a little bit of money down which was all I had. My father had fallen on hard times, and we didn't have any money and so I convinced this fella to finance this business for me.

And it was just $500 a month worth of business. So then I called my friend Herman, well my father's friend Herman Molder, and I said Herman I want to come to Chicago and see you. So I got on a plane and I flew to Chicago and I said Herman I'm going to leave, I bought this business in Fort Lauderdale, and I want to buy your business. And he said, OK, I want $35,000 for my business, plus take over the leases on the trucks, and I said OK, I'll do that. And he said, "where are you going to get the money?" And I said "you're going to finance me", and he laughed and laughed and after we talked for a while he said, I'll tell you what I'm going to do. I'm going to sell you the business, no money down. I'm going to finance you, but get this straight, I'm not doing this for you, I'm doing it because your father and I were friends for a long time, and I want to help you out because of your father. I said fair enough. So in the span of a couple of days I bought a commercial route in Fort Lauderdale and 3 residential routes up in Pompano.

And so there I was with no money, and had to run the business. That's how it got started. But it wasn't because I had a vision. It wasn't because I wanted to be in the trucking business or the garbage business or anything like that. It just was a coincidence...

It didn't end there for Wayne. Even the Blockbuster story is a...well, a blockbuster:

I like the recurring revenue concept. I liked the service businesses, so I was going to take all of these service businesses public. While we were at Waste Management we had built up quite a good relationship with Merrill Lynch so one day, I got a phone call from my friend, John Melk. John Melk was President of Waste Management International. He and I've been friends for a long time.... So John Melk called me one day and he said "Wayne, I just helped a friend of mine's son who wanted to be in the video rental business. I loaned him some money as a limited partner in a Blockbuster Video store," and he said, "Wayne, this thing has your name all over it. This is the kind of deal that you should be in." He said you should see the store. I thought "video rental, you got to be kidding me". There is no way, and so I said, no, John, I have zero interest in the video business. For three months he would call me every couple of days and say, "Wayne, I'm telling you, this is your kind of deal, you have to do this." Well my friend John didn't know that I did not own a VCR. I had never rented a video, I'd never been in a video store.

Not a high tech kind of guy, I suggested.

No, and my vision of a of a video store was one of those adult rental places. One day when I was going home at night I saw a guy coming out the side door of this video store and low and behold it was Alan Becker. {laugh} You know my life was changed forever. {Laughing} So anyway, I flew to Chicago to meet with Merrill Lynch to take all these companies public that I had assembled. All these service companies, the bottled water, the laundry. The company was just going to be a publicly held service company. In the meantime, my friend John Melk called my office in Fort Lauderdale and my secretary, knowing that we were good friends, told John, I was there in Chicago. He went to Merrill Lynch and I had already left to visit some other friends while I was in Chicago.

When I got back to the airport, he was waiting for me and he said, "you're not going home until I show you my video store". So I got in the car with him, drove over to the video store.

When I got out of the car and I saw that video store, walked inside and said, "wow, this is something else". In the meantime the fella that had the franchise, a young lad by the name of Scott Beck had the franchise, brought over all the numbers for their stores. There wasn't much history, they were just starting up, so they had all of these projections. Well you and I know what projections are, right? So we had all these projections, so I grabbed up all of these projections for the number of stores they were going to build in Chicago and the numbers on that particular store. All the way home I went through these numbers on the airplane. Next morning I got my guys together. {I} said, "listen, take a look at this here". So we studied the numbers for probably 4 hours, and we said that if these numbers are only half right, this is a heck of a business.

At the time there were 8 Blockbuster stores, mostly in the Dallas area.

I think there were 6 or 7 in Dallas, 1 in Chicago and maybe 1 in Texas some place else, San Antonio or something like that. So we flew to Dallas and met with the Chairman. It was a public company, a small public company. We met with the CEO and founder. His name was David Cook, and we wanted a franchise for the State of Florida. He said, "well, I'd like to do that he said but Orlando's already gone, Tampa's gone, Jacksonville's gone, you can have Fort Lauderdale if you want and Miami but that's all we have left". I said naugh, that's not...So we stayed around and we ended up having dinner with David Cook that night. Over dinner we bought control of this public company. Now I get a lot of credit in life for being the visionary, for the one that thought of the concept. I even get credit sometimes for being the founder, and I wasn't the founder either, but it's a good example again of being in the right place at the right time and getting credit that you really don't deserve . If it wasn't for my friend John Melk and his insistence, we would have never been involved in Blockbuster.

John had a piece of the company and he was involved for a while. I still had these other business, and I now had to sell those off and I sold pieces. I sold all those business off to different companies. The bottled water company went to Clorox and uniform company went to National Linen and so forth. We just sold them off and while we were doing that John even went to Dallas for a while to oversee the thing while we were growing. John played a key role in changing the franchise agreements and doing all that kind of stuff. We are still real good friends. We laugh and joke about it a lot. So it's just another example of being in the right place at the right time and getting credit that you really don't deserve.

*So we've been in lots of different businesses and they all have similar stories and the long and short of it is, you know **once you fall into the opportunity, you have to take advantage of that and make something happen.** When we were at Blockbuster my experience at Waste Management taught me how to work through people and when you have businesses operating in the United States and all around the World, you soon realize that you can't do it yourself. You have to do a lot of things over the telephone, you have to hire the right people, put them in the right place. You have to be able to communicate and you can't communicate eye ball to eye ball. You have to communicate over the telephone a lot of times. When we decided to see Blockbuster, we said hey, this is really great, this is something that is special here. So if we don't move quick, there was nothing proprietary, so if we don't move quick somebody else is really going to build these things out. So we set up 8 regions around the United States, we hired 8 regional vice presidents, 8 real estate guys, 8 construction guys, the whole thing. We spent a lot money setting up the organization and over 6 years we averaged opening a new Blockbuster store every 17 hours.... And so that was a rapid growth for us, and we bought back a lot of franchisees because the franchise agreements they had signed prior to us, they were not the right kind of franchise agreements. So we had to buy them back. We ended up having some franchises and we had to franchise these mostly in small towns. We bought the franchise back in the bigger towns and had those for ourselves.*

It became a household name, no doubt about that.   When   we sold there were a little over 4,000 Blockbuster stores. When we bought the company, the market value of this small public company was $32 million dollars and 7 years later we sold it for $8.5 billion.

Unfortunately my percentage had declined along the way. You know, we got diluted.
Well, I said, I guess you have to take the good with the bad.
We're not complaining.
No, I guess not.

Bob Graham, former Governor of Florida and U.S. Senator:

I was elected [to the Florida State Legislature] when I was 29. But that fact is just part of a little family story. My mother and father made 2 very big decisions in February of 1936. The first decision was that my father, who was a mining engineer by education, had come to South Florida to be an engineer with a sugar cane operation. He stayed after the depression and went into dairy business, which his family had been in back in Michigan. He had some interest in politics, but it certainly wasn't the driving force in his life; but he became so disgusted at the level of corruption in Dade County, particularly that of some pretty major league underworld figures, like Al Capone who lived here. And it was beginning to affect his own business. His truck drivers, for instance, were being held up and forced to pay heavy unwarranted fines and if they didn't pay up, the milk would be thrown out.

So with that motivation, he said I'm going to run for the Florida State Senate. This was at a time when there was no home rule and a State Senator could exercise a lot of control over the County and the Cities within the County that they represented. Second decision he made was that they would have a baby and I was the product of the second decision. So I spent all of my gestation going to political events and I was born on November the 9th, the same week that my father was elected to the State Senate. So I've had the good fortune since most elections are in early November, I had been able to celebrate an election victory and a birthday almost simultaneously for a number of years.

Brad Meltzer, novelist, suggested that opportunities just fell in front of him. But, I observed, of course you have to recognize them when they cross your path. He said,

Of course you have to. You can't just walk past them, but at the same time they still have to cross your path and some people will call whatever…I think I do believe God is definitely with me on that level. Has put all these different things in front of me to trip over, and maybe I'm just stupid enough that I keep falling, but I really just don't think it's just my, my wonderful brain and my fantastic imagination that's got me do the things I've been able to do. I just think that there are, you know…I grew up in Brooklyn, New York and when we lived in Brooklyn, it was in a very middle class neighborhood. When I was going there I didn't think I was ever going to go to college when I was growing up there. I thought you went to work after high school. That's what I thought people did and when I was 13 years old, my Dad moved down to Florida, started his life over at the age of 40. He had $1,200 to his name.

That was pretty gutsy, I said.

Yes, he was pretty gutsy. I mean I learned from the best, and he basically started his life over. I remember going to the first job interview he ever had, and we didn't have a babysitter so we actually went to the job interview with him. It was in a Wendy's, and I remember that he was being interviewed on the opposite side of the Wendy's, for this insurance job. I remember sitting there picking up my french fries and we were pretending that we didn't know who he was because obviously you don't bring your kids to the job interview.

I was 13 years, I guess I was 14 years old at that point and I remember sitting there thinking my life is being decided on the other end of this dumb Wendy's. And here I'm picking at these fries and my fate's being decided on the opposite side of this restaurant. And when I look back on it, I mean, my parents lied about my address, so that I could go the wealthy suburban high school, public school. When I went to that school, suddenly people were talking about this thing called college, and they were asking about the SATs and what I was going to do. I didn't even know what the SATs were, I had no idea. But because we moved to this area and because my parents sent me to this school, suddenly this whole world opened for me and now I was, wow everyone else is going to college, I better go to college. And, again, that had nothing to do with me. That was just the circumstances I was put in.

And that's it. I look back at it...Recently I saw some friends who I grew up with in Brooklyn, and I look back and they showed me the old yearbook and they were showing me pictures of all my friends in Brooklyn and you know, none of my friends, none of my friends that were in Brooklyn went to a school like Michigan. Not that Michigan is the greatest school in the whole world, but some of them didn't even go to college, some of them didn't do anything. Some of them did go to college and some of them did become lawyers. But I just was like, gosh, this could have been my life also. It was like looking at the life that you never lived in but you easily could have, and again I just think, you know those are things that are out of your control.

Clarence Otis, CEO, Darden Restaurants, grew up in the Watts section of Los Angeles, a poor African American area, shortly after the race riots that devastated that community. I suggested to Clarence that growing up in Watts during that period could have affected him and his life very differently from the way it did.

You are right. I mean, there are in a community like Watts, a lot of different things you can get into...a lot of distractions, a lot of disfunctionality. But in that community, beyond my parents, you had a lot of people who were dedicated to making sure there were possibilities. A lot of those folks were teachers, a lot of them were associated with programs in the community, some athletic, who had full time jobs, who worked with us. A team of Afro-Americans. I grew up down the street from Watts Towers. They had an art center associated with that run by a good visual artist.

The Watts Tower Program...Mrs. Henderson, who played the mother on Julia...I remember that. And they exposed us, not just to the programs in the community; they took us out of community. I remember the first time I ever saw a fairly impressive house was when she had a party for the kids who participated in the program, and all of those things were telling us that we could achieve, that we could be part of a world that was different than the one that we're in. In addition, I have a sister that's a year older, a sister that's a year younger, and my older sister was always a good student, a role model for that, so we did well in school. We did well in elementary school, and it became clear that we could go to college, and then it became increasingly clear that we could go to a selected college if we continued to do it.

Nina Tassler, President, CBS Entertainment:

When my husband and I graduated from college, we were both actors and we moved to New York City to work in the theater and that was the whole end goal. Ironically I think I tested for a soap opera as an actress when I got out of college and was working in the theater. We were working off Broadway at the time and we didn't have aspirations. We didn't have a sense of what television was and, if anything when you come up and you're working in the theater, you look at TV as a little bit of a sell out—you look at TV as sort of you're settling for something and you have what we call sort of a little bit of a "theater snobbery". We just never expected to end up working in television. If it wasn't for my husband, who was testing for a sitcom right after we got married, I would never have come out to California and it was his decision to move to California. I never would have thought of going into TV.

I didn't have a job and I needed one so I had one friend out here. My roommate from college lived here and was an actress. She was actually doing OK at the time. I went to an employment agency, and I remember I went and interviewed for a job as the Assistant to the Import/Export President of the Import/Export Division of the Thrifty Drug Stores, and I had to take a typing test. I will never forget, and in those days you had to type on carbon, so if you made a mistake, you couldn't just do the correcting key, they would literally count how many mistakes you made, and I was like a 55 word per minute typist. Not a great typist, and I interviewed for a job as a receptionist at the Irv Schechter Agency, which was a Talent Agency.

That was not exactly what you had in mind? I asked.

No, not at all, not at all. I mean I was working with a theater company, the Pacific Repatory Theater Company in Venice at the time. Friends of mine had started a theater company there. So I was working with them, but I needed a job, I needed an income. I remember it was a Thursday or Friday afternoon where I had those 2 interviews. One was for the receptionist job. I'd have to answer telephones plus be an assistant to two agents. And I remember coming home feeling so depressed and so dejected, because I had taken the typing test and by the time I got home, I remember walking up the walkway, my husband and I were renting a house up in Hollywood Hills, and I remember walking by the window to a bedroom and my husband said "there's a phone call for you". It turned out to be the talent agent with whom I interviewed and he said "you're hired, can you come in on Monday"? I said "thank God, I got the job" and I started work on that Monday. I got the call Monday afternoon that I got the job with Thrifty. So I thought, "thank God, I could have ended up working for the Import/ Export Department at Thrifty".

Influence of Parents

Yes, events shape our lives, but few things have a greater effect on us than do our parents. If you were burdened with parents who were absent, or who were unhappy, who were not ambitious—for themselves or for you—or did not believe in the possibilities the world holds for each of us, it is far more difficult to succeed than if you have supportive parents who believe in you and believe in the possibilities for future. It is certainly not impossible, just more difficult, requiring you to learn and apply the lessons that follow in later chapters. The lessons would be the same if you have supportive parents, but the leap of faith in accepting them is not quite so great. Many of the super-successful people I interviewed attributed their opportunities, attitudes and ambitions to their parents.

I found it interesting that while most did, in some way, consider their family important to their success, the men tended to refer to their mother and father, while the women tended to attribute the greatest influence to the support from their fathers.

Madeleine Albright, former Secretary of State:

*I've written in my memoir that **the thing about my parents that was so interesting, was that they made the abnormal seem normal**. We had gone through so many ups and downs, and so many moves, and they made it seem as if that was kind of a normal life, and they themselves worked very very hard. My father, who had been* *an Ambassador and I remember so well, living in an Embassy and all kinds of butlers and chauffeurs and everything, and then **we came to the United States and we basically had nothing. He had to start a career over and persevered** in teaching and writing in a foreign language. My mother, who had been a daughter out of a fairly well to do family, as I said, had already learned to take care of everything and work hard when we were in England during the War, but then we came to the United States, she went to work as a secretary. **They both persevered very hard and they basically, in looking back on it, were pretty upbeat about everything and very grateful to be here.** So their approach to everything, I think, really made the difference. I mean, we were just so glad to be here, that was the main thing.*

So, I said, gratitude for what you have and optimism are key features of what you learned from your parents about being successful?

*Very much so, and I think understanding that **you aren't owed something. That you have to earn it, and that being a part of a society that allows you to do that is very important.** I remember my father saying something to the effect that in Europe there is this whole class of people that they call the "Intelligencia" and, at least in the time that he was growing up, he said, and also in his life, the Intelligencia never worked with their hands. And he was so interested that when he became a college Professor here to find his students pumping gas or waiting on tables. He was so impressed with the fact that in America that's what people did, and so he never, we never fell into what we might of fallen into in Europe, of being part of the Intelligencia that never did this kind of thing. So we all worked. When I was in high school, I worked in a department store and my mother worked and then later my brother and sister. So I think we kind of took the best out of Europe and combined it with what we saw as the best of America.*

Jeb Bush, Governor of Florida, commenting on my question about public reports that his Mother advised her Grandchildren to first make their money and then do their public service, said:

Well, I think in public life the folks that make it a career from the git go, and they want a career in politics, and I would say that the best way to have a career in politics is to be successful in something else so that you can add value to the political process. The people that make it a career end up failing, based on what I can see. I haven't done a scientific study of it. Gosh, you know the best legislators and the best people in public life are the ones that have a unique perspective because they've had an experience that they bring to the political process. It think that is what my Mom was saying: be a good Husband, be successful in business or be a good lawyer or a good doctor or be a community leader and then aspire to public life because then you have something that you can share. If you want to be a politician when you are 21 years old, then you can work your way up the ladder I guess, but it's a pretty static way of being involved in public service. In fact it isn't public service, it's service to yourself.

I asked him if being from a family of high achievers put pressure on him:

*No, I mean we are very competitive but it is not in a hurtful way. **I think being competitive and having an edge to you to want to achieve things is really good, but you can go beyond that where it clogs your judgement or it impedes your ability to be a person of good character.** So I've never felt pressured to do much. I've always been pretty independent. It's one of the things my parents did teach me, at least my Mother or both of them, my Mom in particular taught me, don't assume things. I was pretty rebellious when I was young and I was encouraged to be, maybe they would admit it now, but to challenge basic assumptions. I think **being successful in whatever you pursue you have to have a healthy—a little bit of disrespect for authority because you have to challenge things and to push things forward. To always assume that it's got to be the way it is is a little dangerous. You kind of get into a rut.** My parents taught me that, maybe more than anything else, that's been helpful in my life, particularly in politics where there are so many stupid things that go on simply because they were they way we do things, because we did them that way yesterday. In the private sector of a real world where life is much more dynamic, you have to change to survive and succeed. In government, you can get inside the bubble, the 'work bosom of government' if you will, and keep doing it the same way and maybe be perceived to be successful.*

Jorge de Cespedes, President of PharMed, when I asked what influences in his life could have accounted for his early entrepreneurial bent (at age 8), said:

> *I think as I look back, certainly my Dad was nothing like an entrepreneur, but my Grandmother...I lived a little compact that I had with her back in the old Country. My Mother's Mother was an entrepreneur. She would buy and sell jewelry and somehow she got her hands on lotto tickets from other countries and sell those. I didn't get to spend a lot time with her, but the last couple years of my life in Cuba, I guess I did spend quite a bit of time, was exposed to a lot of that.*

Bob Graham, former Florida Governor and U.S. Senator, when I asked him what was the best life advice he had received, told me:

> *My father would be the origin of the advice. One piece of advice that he gave that I followed and another piece of advice that I rejected. The part I followed, he was a great believer in families.* **To not only be successful, but also to have an enjoyable life.** *You should encourage families to stick together and I will say that our business has practiced rampant nepotism where 4 or 5 of his offspring are in the business. My youngest daughter was here until she just had a couple babies and I think when they get a little older she'll probably come back. That has not only contributed to our company, which started off as a dairy farm and now we're still very much in the dairy business and a lot of other business.* [ASB: One of the biggest development companies.]

> *Yeah, because we got members of the family running almost every division of the company. The second piece of advice that I didn't follow. Dad was in politics and was sort of a believer in the school that said, don't get mad, get even. He kept a list in his mind of at least of the people he had a bad experience with and that finally was the undoing of his political career. I've adopted and believed just because you're a political competitor you don't have to be engaged in a blood sport. In fact among the most enjoyable parts of my political life have been that the people who I ran against, and this goes all the way back to the legislature, but in particular people like Bob Shevin, Bruce Smathers, Hans Tanzler, Jim Williams, you know Claude Kirk, we were all*

running for Governor in 1978, as well as Jack Eckert who was a Republican. I would count all of them as my friends and have a good relationship with Paula Hawkins [who Graham beat in his first race for US Senate] and I think it's important in politics to not end up with a long string of scalps of your adversaries, but to end up with a holiday greetings list that has your former political opponents listed as folks that you want to stay in touch with.

Brad Meltzer, novelist:

My family, the most amazing thing of all, is my family couldn't afford where I decided to go to college, and I don't think that's very different than many families in America. The difference was, my parents didn't try to stop me, and they knew that when I wanted to go to the University of Michigan that it was going to stretch them beyond any reasonable point, and they still said I should go. "You should go to the best school you get into and we'll figure it out later," and, you know, maybe that's a smart decision, maybe it's a completely dumb financial decision, but they let me follow that dream wherever it was going to take me and for that alone I'll never be able to repay them. As far as law school, again, I was the first in my immediate family to go to a four year college and so when I was growing up my Dad once said to me "whatever grades you get in school are going to be better than the ones I got, so, fantastic work". I guess the fact that we were bringing home grades that were, that maybe were better than that, I think we were shocked by it and it felt like, ok it's fantastic!

On how he might pass along to his children the lessons he has learned, Brad said,

so much of {success} is that you have a little bit of nurture, but you have so much nature. I think on some level you are born almost completely developed and then it's just up to the parents to mess us up or raise us a little better than what they're delivered with and I think obviously that's a lesson I hope I can relay. That will be a wonderful one to relay.

Clarence Otis, CEO, Darden Restaurants:

I think {my parents} did have aspirations for their kids. I think that was part of the whole dream of what they would define as success, is *that they could have their kids reach levels that they couldn't. So even though they had visions for themselves, and they achieved that…my father was a janitor who became head of maintenance at Los Angeles airport…so getting back to their kids, **they clearly expected one of those markers for kids would be college education and whatever doors that would open up, that would make the possibilities for the kids bigger than they were for them.***

They didn't so much talk about college as they did achieving in school. I don't know that they knew enough about how it all worked. But they kind of knew if you did well, then you increased your chances. So it was really important. You've got to go to school. Do everything you could do after the riot; not just the riot but the whole Watts experience.

Susan Story, CEO, Gulf Power Co.:

*Well, when I was very young, my Mom and Dad both worked in a cotton mill. My Dad was a lab tech and my Mom was on an assembly line. And then when I was 7, my Dad got a job as a pipefitter, which was a craft that he was able to make more money at, and my Mother was able to stay home. We lived paycheck to paycheck. It was the type of home where we didn't have a lot of money, but home was the safe, fun, happy place. My brother and I were my parents' top priority, and we played games together, we laughed together. Home was that place where you were fully accepted for what you were, and were encouraged. My Dad is a very bright man, and he came from an alcoholic home, joined the Marines at 17, after he'd been living on the streets for 2 years; joined the Marines to straighten his life out. My Mom was the youngest of 9 kids of a poor farmer. **And so our life was, you work hard, you don't feel sorry for yourself, you never take.** I mean, we never were on welfare or anything like that. If my Dad had to work 3 jobs, and my Mom did too, that's what they did and we always had food on the table. My Mom and Dad were also the kind…I remember in high school, I was very popular and was a favorite, and Home Coming and all this stuff, and I always had as nice a dress as anybody else did. My Mom would go a year without buying anything herself, so that I could have a dress at a ball. That's the kind of people they were. We were—my brother and I, were the most important things in their lives, but they didn't spoil us. They couldn't monetarily. But they* *wanted us to grow up to be responsible adults. The best gift I got from Dad was he really believed in this Country. Grew up in a horrible home situation, but joined the military. It changed his life. He was a Marine, is a Marine, somebody told me once you're never "was" a Marine, you're always a Marine, once a Marine, enlisted Marine. And his hope was that in this Country you can do and be everything you can be. And the life that he and my Mom gave my brother and me was far better than what either one of them had. They said, there are no boundaries to what you can do. And I grew up with my Dad saying, "you can be and do anything you want to be", and I believed him. I mean, I believed him.*

She also believed the lessons about work:

Working hard. You know, we had chores around the house. I cut grass and worked in the garden, and we did all these things and we were very responsible. When I was 16, I worked on weekends at a little photo shop. It wasn't a lot of money, but it was enough to get me a little spending money. We just grew up taking a lot of personal responsibility.

It was her father's encouragement that led her to a field not populated by many women: engineering:

My Dad has a really good math and science mind, and so as a kid, my Dad would play all of these games with me and my younger brother. And one of them is this game called Crypto. We were like 6 and 7 years old, and you take cards and you get 5 cards in your hand and then they turn a card up and you multiply, add, subtract and divide to come up with a number and see who can do that fastest. We did all these math mind games that my Dad played with us. So it became very easy for us to do math and I loved math. I loved science and I just had this natural curiosity about why is the world the way it is. So I started as a math major. The little high school I went to in rural Alabama, it's about 240 in my graduating class, but they didn't think women ought to be engineers either. So they never told me about being an engineer. I went to college and I talked to them, and they said "you really ought to look at engineering. You can make a good living and it plays to your strengths." And I went into it, and you're right, there were very, very few woman, but interestingly the woman who were there tended to be at the top of the class.

Nina Tassler, President, CBS Entertainment:

I was raised in a family atmosphere and in an environment where my parents, really instilled in me a sense of quality, a sense of decency, a sense of human rights and that anything I set out to do in my life, if I worked hard, and I paid the price, then I should have it. "Pay the price" meaning if I worked hard in school, if I got the grades, if I did that, I would succeed. That I should accomplish. That I was entitled to whatever dreams, whatever ambition I had, that I should have those things because of the fact that I'm their daughter and those are the things that I should have in life and, ironically, and I think I mentioned this to you before, my parents paid very little attention to the actual physical aspects of things that I accomplished. Their emphasis was more on—did I personally feel a sense of accomplishment. Did I personally feel that I had worked as hard or that I had devoted as much time and energy to a particular assignment or task or goal that I should have and that I should value those things for myself and not for them.

Not only her family's values, but possibly her father's career, had an influence on Nina's destiny:

*I have to tell you, my father worked at CBS in 1955 in New York City before I was born and then after I was born we moved to Long Island, and he was commuting from Long Island to the City, which was tough on him, so he left the company at that time. There was also apparently a threat of a pending strike and he was one of the newer people hired so he figured he would be one of the first people to let go, and he was recently married and had a child, so he decided to leave the company. So in a weird way, I was raised with CBS being, for most of my life, the network that we watched. I was raised on Walter Cronkite. These were shows that I heard about. I watched Captain Kangaroo, so in truth it was the first network I was ever introduced to. In that way **I wouldn't be surprised if fate played some hand in my being at this company today.***

Burdens and Benefits for Women and Minorities

We have all heard how much more difficult it is for women or minorities to achieve success. There are undoubtedly roadblocks along the way, ingrained attitudes in our society and in the workplace, that sometimes make it more difficult to achieve. Yet, all of our super-successful women and minorities figured it out. In some instances they fought the prejudices that have held back others; in some instances they learned to use their uniqueness to their advantage.

I asked **Madeleine Albright** if she had encountered difficulties as a woman, and if she had problems being taken seriously as a person who is a female and short (she proclaims: *"I'm 5'2"...well, actually 5'1 and ¾"*). She replied,

> *It is funny, the short part never entered as an issue, but it did in one way, I'll get back to it. But here again, I think **my father had a very large role in this because I was the oldest child and there was never anything that he said that would indicate that I couldn't do something because I was a girl.** The school I went to was a girl's school and then I went to a women's college, and so, you had to be a good person on the student council or the editor of the newspaper or whatever, so I really came out of a climate where women, my role models, were a lot of the professors or the teachers. And my father. I didn't have a lot of other role models, but when I got out of college, I immediately hit the woman problem. I did get married right away. I went to apply for one of my first jobs, when we moved to Chicago I wanted to be a journalist. And my husband was a journalist. We were having dinner with his managing editor and he said to me "so what are you going to do, honey" and I said "well I want to work on another newspaper". There were four newspapers in Chicago at the time. He said, "well, like, why would you want to do that?" and I said "well, that's my career that I've chosen. I've already worked on a small newspaper in Missouri while he was in the Army". And he said, "well you can't work on the same paper as your husband because there are guild relations that prevent that and you certainly wouldn't want to compete with him, so I suggest you try another career". It was '59, '60 and I just saluted and said "yes". I then went and found another job at Encyclopedia Britannica where I*

*was asked whether I intended to get pregnant right way. So that was the kind of things, in contrast to how people feel now, would ask any of those questions. You know I basically went along with the program. So for a long time I think that internally, in terms of the way I've been brought up, **I never felt there were any issue about doing things that I wanted to as a woman. But I certainly ran into problems very early** and then, something that I say with great sadness, is that some of my problems when I was having children and getting my Ph.D. and doing a lot of other things, some of the problems were other woman who would say, "well you know, are you spending enough time with your children?", "how do you think they feel if you're not in the carpool line?" or whatever.*

So, I asked, a lot of woman felt that you had to make a choice, and if you try to do both, you couldn't do that?

*Right, and I think that that was my era. Now, my daughters are grown up and we have lots of discussions about this. **It's not exactly simple to be a woman and have children and be married and have a job and do all those things. And I actually think that you don't have to make all the choices all at once.** There are advantages to being a woman in terms of that our life comes in segments dictated by biology, and you don't have to do everything all at once. And the thing I think that is so important for woman and men is that as we make choices about what we're going to do, I think it's important to realize that there's no one pattern.... Also this is very much advice to young woman, to not decide doing some chore is beneath you. I made a lot of coffee, I did a lot of Xeroxing and a lot of things that I thought that somebody with a Ph.D. didn't need to do and yet, I think that being cheerful, willing and able, is very, very important. No, I told this to so many of my kids and their friends: no redwoods on your shoulder. You don't go in being irritated about something that you expect to happen to you. Now, on the short issue—high heels are great. Very much into high heels. I've never felt short, I've mostly felt fat, but not short. But what was very funny is, when I went to speak to a Girl Scout troop, there was a little girl who looked up at me and she said "but you're so little" and I think that the thing that surprised them is because I'd done so much TV and I was out there as a big major* *figure, all of the sudden I was this little person. I think that kind of surprised them.*

Jorge de Cespedes, President of PharMed and part owner of Charlotte Bobcats:

> [Owning an NBA team] *is a thrill. That's a thrill and going forward, each win becomes your win. You want to be able to actually, work with a guy like Bob Johnson* [founder of BET and Jorge's partner in the Bobcats] *and you know we are very very very similar. He tells a story that we have a lot of things in common: I escaped from Cuba and he escaped from Mississippi.*

I asked **Clarence Otis,** CEO, Darden Restaurants, if he found, as an African-American man, that there were any impediments or advantages to his advancement in business:

> *I think there are both. I think that as an African-American you're noticed. Because there aren't a lot of African-Americans in the room, at that level, and that's a real advantage because in a corporate organization, one of the big obstacles is getting noticed* [laugh]. *When you're, especially as an entry level person, but even as a middle manager, and so the fact that you are able to stand out is an advantage. Then, of course, there is what do you do with the fact that you're noticed. Do you take advantage of it? To put a great foot forward. So, I think those are advantages actually. I think on the disadvantage side, as people are thinking about the next level, they haven't seen a person like you at that level, so they need to overcome that sort of "haven't really seen it before" kind of sense. I think it's a natural tendency even when people have very good intentions, it's just—and I think that's an issue for women—in a lot of places, just haven't seen them in similar situations in their mind's eye and so you have to get past that hurdle.*

By doing a good job? I asked.

> *Yup, yup, and running into people who are open minded. Who don't make a lot of assumptions. You know, I'd say to think about Joe Lee, who I worked for here at Darden, who I'm succeeding in the CEO slot. Joe is a person who doesn't make assumptions about anything. He's open to hear and look at facts: what do we know? What do we not know? What have we a pretty good idea about.... He doesn't*

jump to conclusions and that carries through when you think about diversity.…

Susan Story, CEO, Gulf Power Co.:

Early in my career as an engineer, I worked for a supervisor who I found out later really did not want me to work for him. Did not think woman ought to be engineers. But, I was performing.

*He would take work I did and take my name off it and put his name on it. He would give mediocre performance ratings when I was doing things that had never been done before, in terms of helping the Power Plant and doing things. And I remember one day I said, "what do I have to do to change my mediocre performance rating?" He said, "nothing, I save the high ratings for the men with families, so that they will get more money." Unbelievable! That was in the early 80s, and of course later his boss found out about it, he got removed from the job. My company's always been great about making sure that doesn't happen. The day I found what he had done, that day that his boss came to me and I said "I don't understand the disparity between your performance that I see and what's written here," and I very, innocently—I was just 22 years old, and it was in 1982, I innocently relayed to him what had been told to me, and his face got red and he was very upset. But when that happened, **I remember saying to myself: you know, I have a choice. It's not about him, it's about me. I can be bitter and I can be cynical and I can blame "the system" or I can sit back and say, you know what—this is his problem, this is not about me,** this is about him, and I am not going to let him effect me and my life and my commitment and what I do. And you know what? Choosing the latter has made all the difference.*

I asked Susan how she had gone into the electric power business, a field not generally known for having many female executives:

I was very fortunate in that there were very few women engineers with the grades I had and the activities I had and I actually had 17 job offers from across the country when I graduated with my engineering degree. From New York to California to the South. Bottom line, I decided to stay in the South to be closer to my Mom and Dad because we've always been a close knit family. And I started working for the

Southern Company, for Alabama Power, as a nuclear power plant engineer. I'm glad, because in an industry like the one I'm in now, having a technical background and coming up through line functions is very important in terms of moving into the top.

And when, I asked, did it occur to you that you might be able to move into the top?

*Wow, that's a great question. Honestly, probably not until I became an officer of one of our subsidiaries in 1993. At that time I was the youngest Vice President ever, within Southern Company, and even then I'm not sure I really thought I would be president, CEO. I guess maybe 9 year ago, 8 years ago, I started thinking, maybe I could do that. This looks like something, the more I became acquainted with what was known...**you kind of look at that these jobs when you grow up when I did, and you think "wow, this person must be the most brilliant person in the world" and then you say, "yeah, they're smart, but they're just like I am." One thing that helped me was continuing education.** Not only do I have an engineering degree and an MBA, my company very much believes in executive education, continuing education. So I went to Duke in 1998 and then the company said, you can go to any executive program, Harvard, MIT, Oxford, wherever you want to go. I looked at the advanced management program they do for senior executives, and I saw that Harvard says half their people are international, but that means half are Americans. I wanted to go to a program where US citizens were not in the majority, because I really thought that would make a difference. So I chose the Oxford program, and out of 36 people in my class; only 3 were US citizens. We were there for 6 weeks. It was a whole different dynamic, being a different country, in a program where you're in the minority, which we're not accustomed to in the US. And as I worked with these folks from across the World, and we still keep contact pretty much, I realized, you know I can hold my own with any of these folks. And when you grow up in rural north Alabama, it helps to become more knowledgeable and worldly, and then I came back and I was in International Woman's forum. I was selected as part of the leadership program. I did studies at Harvard and Cambridge. Went to Israel, and also DC for further training. We have a reunion this group of women, 11 women. We're scattered* *out, Cary Schwab Pomerance (Charles Schwab's daughter), a senior executive in New York City, a bio-medical engineer from Houston who works with all of this space shuttle tests that they do in space. It's just a neat close knit group of women. And after we went through that year together, it was four full weeks within that year, we still have a reunion every year. We're meeting in San Francisco in April, in fact and we meet somewhere every year just to come and reconnect. So, it's not one thing that said "gee you could become this"—I think it's a series of experiences that give you the confidence that says, "you know, this is a good thing and I can bring value".*

Nina Tassler, President, CBS Entertainment has made it to the top in Hollywood, perhaps one of the most male chauvinist business arenas in the world. Yet, today, she and a number of other very successful women hold lead positions. I asked her if being a woman poses any special opportunities or challenges, and if things have changed in Hollywood:

Firstly, my boss is notorious for being the biggest supporter of promoting women within each division of the company.

I observed that she has family and young children. As a woman, she obviously has to balance a lot. How, I asked, do you do that balancing act?

*It's a challenge, I haven't perfected it yet. But I realize my children are my priority and **it requires a tremendous amount of planning and organization** and, you know, it's very important to me that I volunteer in my daughter's classroom; it's important to me that I'm on committees at my son's school. It's also important to my family that I participate in other philanthropic organizations because I want my children to understand that this should be a part of their lives growing up as well. It's a challenge and there are times we have to make a lot of sacrifices but much of life is about, um, life is about negotiation, life is about establishing priorities and my children know that they are my priority. They know that when it comes time to make a costume, when it comes time to be at the school for one of their functions, I am always there and I am involved with my son's SAT Prep Classes, his tutors, his whatever. Whatever parts of their life are important to them are important to me. I don't think you ever achieve sort of the perfect balance, but I've learn to sort of take one day at a time.*

Yet, in such a busy life, something has to give. For Nina, it is relaxation.

I don't relax. I don't really have much time to myself. It eludes me, quite frankly, how to do it. I mean, it's also about this time in my life. My youngest is 6 and is still at a time in her life where my involvement and my care as a mother are my priority. I have my children, my husband, and my family, work, there really isn't much time to myself. I used to play more golf than I do now and between the two kids, I used to be able to play a lot more, and I'll eventually get back to playing more.

Both my kids have spent time in my office. Any function that I have to go to through the network, they're there. Parties, they're there, and my son, who is older, he's 17, is at an age when we have to go to the Grammy's or we recently did a special on Ray Charles, we were able to go to the show, and I took my son, his friend and his friend's Mom. It was just a really fun night and he enjoys that and he shares that with me and he likes being a part of it. The little one, my daughter, is still a little too young to appreciate it. I mean it just happens that my son enjoys all of that stuff, but they are very comfortable coming to the office. I've worked with some of the same people for over 15 years. So they've watched me, they've watched the kids grow up, they've been there for the Bar and Bat Mitzvahs, the baby namings, for all of that, so it's a little bit like a family environment. They make them very comfortable coming there.

As Clarence Otis had mentioned about minorities, it takes open-minded executives to recognize and promote women to the positions of responsibility they deserve. In Nina's case, that Chief Executive is Les Moonves.

*My boss has always been at the forefront, not only supporting, but promoting women to positions of leadership and power in whatever company he was working. At one point, when he was the President at Warner Brothers Television, I think every major department was run by a women and those were people that he had put in place. He is always very comfortable. He is a believer, obviously in equal rights, but he populates his company with creative woman, strong women. **I found that within my generation, they were a group of women who*** *basically felt very comfortable with their priorities in that they wanted families, they wanted their careers, they knew it wasn't going to be easy to have both, but they weren't willing to sacrifice one for the other. As a result, many friends of mine with kids are successful women and are either running companies, running divisions, independent producers, or so on. Their kids are incredibly well equipped to go out in the world. They're socially sophisticated, they're comfortable in a multitude of settings. They're articulate, they have great social skills, and I think that they are also boys or girls who look at their mothers who are in the work place and without it being taught to them, they have a sense of equality. I know my son is that way. But probably about half a generation before me were women who had to make a different series of sacrifices. Perhaps women who said "if I want my career, I can't have kids" or "if I want my career I can't have a husband." But I would say that pretty consistent with my generation are women who are very dedicated to having it all.*

Of course, as with many successful women, her parents directed her toward success.

I was raised in a family atmosphere and in an environment where my parents, really instilled in me a sense of quality, a sense of decency, a sense of human rights and that anything I set out to do in my life, if I worked hard, and I paid the price, then I should have it. "Pay the price" meaning if I worked hard in school, if I got the grades, if I did that, I would succeed. That I should accomplish. That I was entitled to whatever dreams, whatever ambition I had, that I should have those things because of the fact that I'm their daughter and those are the things that I should have in life and, ironically, and I think I mentioned this to you before, my parents paid very little attention to the actual physical aspects of things that I accomplished. Their emphasis was more on—did I personally feel a sense of accomplishment. Did I personally feel that I had worked as hard or that I had devoted as much time and energy to a particular assignment or task or goal that I should have and that I should value those things for myself and not for them.

As we can see, all of the super-successful people I spoke with have had experiences that shaped their lives, in some cases building their strength to face the vagaries of life. Many had the good fortune to enjoy parental support, which mostly provided the critical element in their success: belief in themselves and their abilities to achieve. But, as we shall see, in practice all were aware, at some level, of the secrets for success which are described in the following chapters. All of them lived by these rules, have found success, and are willing to share their insights and experiences so that you too will find the fulfillment and success to which you are entitled.

CHAPTER 4
THE FIRST SECRET: THE TWO STEPS TO SUCCESS

To anyone reading the best-selling (not necessarily the best) books about achieving success, losing weight, self improvement, playing the piano or just about anything else, it would appear that there is a formula that requires the result be broken into a distinct number of component parts; not more than ten nor less than five. Good examples in the success genre are Stephen Covey's *The 7 Habits of Highly Effective People* and Stuart Levine's *The Six Fundamentals of Success* (despite the unexciting titles, both are worthwhile reads), and Deepak Chopra's *The Seven Spiritual Laws of Success*. The prevailing approach—at least of publishers and marketers—is that the consuming public wants to buy its practical advice in distinct bite size pieces. Naturally, it is possible to expand any concept or subdivide it sufficiently to meet this mandated objective. Clearly, the subtitle of this book is an homage to the publishing industry.[5]

At the grave risk of being accused of over simplifying, I have always believed that achieving success is indeed relatively simple, and in fact, has just **two simple but necessary steps**. That is not to say that each isn't susceptible to more detailed analysis, but the essential steps come down to this:

Step 1: Set a goal.

Step 2: Do it.

While we can endlessly debate the essentials of what it takes to set a viable goal, there can be no achievement without starting with the goal. I will discuss in greater detail in a later chapter the importance of belief in what you want and in what you can be, but by whatever process you get there, you must first have a goal. While this might seem self-evident, all you have to do is look around you and you will see many people running around expending huge amounts of energy in the pursuit of....

of what? They are not sure. They are too busy doing, and never took time to reflect what the end game will be. They have not stopped to ask: what is success for me? What is the state I want to reach in my personal life or business life? What do I have to do to get there? What must I give up and what must I focus more attention on? Instead, they are busy all the time dealing with a million distractions. Family demands. Day-to-day business activities. Leisure activities—oh, there always seems to be time for leisure. Saddest of all, many people use up enormous amounts of time and energy just thinking about what they do not have or have not accomplished.

The place to start with goal setting is to suspend activity for a while. Stop and **take time to reflect**. What do I really want? Not the top one hundred things, but the top one thing. There is almost nothing you cannot do if you set your goal and then methodically go about achieving it.

When my older daughter was a junior in college she called me one day and seemed troubled. "I am really concerned because I am entering my last year of college and I don't know what I want to do. I have no special burning passion, something I must be or accomplish."

My response: "OK."

"But," she said, "Aren't you worried that I don't have a goal?"

"No," I truthfully told her. "If you were not worried, I would be worried about it, but since you are worried about it I am not. Keep an open mind and spirit and you will find your goal."

A few months later she told me she was considering going to law school. She was concerned, though, that she would go to law school for the wrong reason: that she had no other good ideas and was just buying time by putting off a working life. I told her there was nothing wrong with filling her time with learning until she found her destiny. So, she began law school the following year. I remember speaking to her during the first couple of weeks. I told her it was no longer enough to get a law degree. The competition among new lawyers was too intense. It was a good idea to couple the law degree with "something else, something that makes you more valuable in a highly specialized world." I mentioned that some of the schools coupled an MBA (Masters of Business Administration) with the law degree (J.D.—Juris Doctor).

A couple of weeks after that she called to tell me she had been accepted in the joint JD/MBA program. "That's great," I said.

"But I am not looking forward to it, because I really hate finance."

"So, why did you apply for it?" I asked.

"Because you told me to!"

"Since when do you do what I tell you to do? If it is not right for you, don't do it. You will find the special something that fits you if you just stay relaxed and open to it when it comes along."

It was not more than a week after that that she had a meeting with the Dean of Students. The meeting was to discuss my daughter's plan to open a peer-counseling center on the law school campus. (By the way, she eventually did organize and operate it after deflecting all the reasons from faculty and the Administration why it could not be done—privacy, training, potential liability, etc. It is a fine example of the points made in a later Chapter about confidence and perseverance.) The Dean asked her, "What do you think you would like to do after law school?" Marni said: "I don't know, but I think I would like your job," she half joked. "Well," replied the Dean, "to do that you would have to have a Masters Degree in Psychology." The very next week my daughter applied to the Masters program at Nova Southeastern University and simultaneous with getting her law degree at the University of Miami, she studied for her Masters in Mental Health Counseling at Nova, some 30 miles away. A high achiever, you might (correctly) observe. But Marni always tells people that even though she was always an A student, her parents never even asked to see her report cards (probably something of an exaggeration), that she accomplished what she did for herself.

The point is, my daughter did not despair of lacking a goal. She continued on a course of learning and exploring until the right thing presented itself, which it almost always will if you give yourself a chance. When the short term goal (attend law school) yielded to longer-term goals, she had found what her destiny was—trial consulting—and went after it with vigor.

You will do far better if you can devote your efforts to furthering your real interests. Celebrity billionaire, Donald Trump, told interviewer extraordinaire Larry King: "Billionaires love what they do. I know people who are miserable with their work. They are never successful." Barbara Goldsmith, biographer of the famous scientist Marie Curie, the first woman to get a physics degree at the Sorbonne in Paris, the first woman appointed a professor at that school, the first woman to win a Nobel Prize (in fact, two of them), wrote this: "While she was determined to make her dream of becoming a scientist come true, she was well aware, she wrote, that 'the way to progress is never swift or easy.' Marie believed that if you **pursue your dream**, things that seem like sacrifices don't really matter."

This point is alluded to in a wonderful little book by Canfield, Hansen and Hewitt (authors of the *Chicken Soup* series) called *The Power of Focus*. They say:

> We are all blessed with a few God-given talents.
> A big part of your life is discovering what these are,
> then utilizing and applying them to the best of
> your ability. The discovery process takes years for
> many people, and some never truly grasp what their
> greatest talents are. Consequently, their lives are
> less fulfilling. These people tend to struggle because
> they spend most of their time in jobs or businesses
> not suited to their strengths.... It doesn't work, and
> it causes a lot of stress and frustration.
>
> * * * *
>
> Setting and achieving goals is one of the best ways to
> measure your life's progress and create unusual
> clarity. Consider the alternative—just drifting along
> aimlessly, hoping that one day good fortune will
> fall in your lap with little or no effort on your part.
> Wake up! You've got more chance of finding a grain
> of sugar on a sandy beach.

I am a big believer in the idea that anything you can dream is possible. However, I am five foot six inches tall. If my dream is to be an NBA basketball player, I might be well advised to readjust my goals. That does not mean I have to write off sports. I could be a sports writer or announcer, a trainer or coach or agent, a manager on the business side of a sports team. If I lack the math gene, perhaps the best path for me would not be a career in rocket science.

Again, in *The Power of Focus*, the authors tell us that the masters only focus on the things they are brilliant at. If you spend too much time working on your weaknesses, you only end up with a lot of strong weaknesses. In other words, you will just be average. A similar point is made in *The 80/20 Individual* by Richard Koch: "If you're not good at something, don't do it....Why work hard to become mediocre at something?"[6]

Billionaire businessman **Wayne Huizenga** made the same point when he explained to me how he deals with issues that come up in his varied business empire:

> *We've had problems along the way. The company which had the most problems was AutoNation. AutoNation today is a $20 billion dollar company. It's a big business, and when you win, you have problems, you have big problems; and there was an example where I hired the wrong person. I hired the right person to make the acquisitions, to grow the business, but it was the wrong person to operate the business. There are people who can do certain things really really well., but they can't do other things well. Some people can grow a business and some people can operate a business. I would say, myself, I'm a better builder than an operator. I can see the vision of how to make something happen and how to be dominant in the marketplace and those types of things, but when it comes to the nitty gritty of operating a business and being really successful and paying close attention to the things that matter, that's not really my strong suit. But that's OK, **if you recognize that's not your strong suit, then you put people in place to do that for you. Where you run into trouble is if you think you can do all things and you don't admit to yourself that you can't do all things.** That, I think, has been, that I think has been good for us and it's been good for a lot of other people too, and the people that are running our businesses today. Whether it's through public services or AutoNation or Extended Stay America, or Boca Resorts, or whatever there are all extremely good people that are running those businesses.*

"What," you may ask, "if I am not brilliant at anything?" Don't sell yourself short. With some introspection you will find something that you excel at or something in which you have a real interest. Perhaps you never thought of how to put those abilities or interests to a practical career use. If necessary, find a professional counselor to help think through it, but I guaranty there will be an ability or interest that you can build on, and build a life on.

Another concern is that before you find the right path, you still have to pay the bills. That is true, but those who let that deter them usually operate under the mistaken belief that their work day consists of just eight hours, or that they can only do one thing at a time. Not so. If you are motivated to reach a goal you will put in whatever time and effort is required.

Of course, there are natural obstacles to many a goal, but the fact that it is very difficult, or that it has not been done before, or that you are the only one who believes it is possible, are not truly impediments to achieving your goal. Many of the great discoveries and accomplishments of our age were achieved by people who did not know (or accept) that it was impossible. More on this in the next chapter.

According to Paul Arden, a British advertising executive and author, nearly all rich and powerful people become rich and powerful by wanting to be rich and powerful. "Your vision of where or who you want to be is the greatest asset you have. Without having a goal, it is difficult to score."

How much does of his success does **Jeb Bush,** Governor of Florida, attribute to goal setting?

*A lot. A whole lot. I think it's important, **it's important to create your own agenda whether it's public realm or private realm and pursue it, and so you have to have a goal and you have to measure how you are doing on that goal.** If you try to be all things to all people and please people, if you always want to respond to other folks' agenda, you'd be overwhelmed, particularly in the job I have now. It would be impossible. So, when I ran in '98 I had a real clear agenda and I said what I was going to do. So it was totally transparent and some people liked it and some people didn't. But then I did or I tried to do what I said I was going to do, which is a novel idea in politics. If I hadn't set the goals and I hadn't articulated what those goals were and how to achieve them, the agenda wouldn't have passed. Now we are kind of at another stage of this. Those goals have* *changed. You accomplish some things, you have to build on those and then new things come up. In our State right now you have the Medicaid budget which grows about 5 times faster than the rest of government and it's just eating away at the ability to fund higher education or community colleges or other needed services. So we have to radically alter our Medicaid program. The last 6 months I have been working on this quietly first and we will establish an aspirational goal of where we need to be and will lay out the plan on how to achieve that goal. I'll try to neutralize the likely opponents and draw people that maybe passive on Medicaid but understand the importance of it because of things that are going in their own life, how it would benefit them; turn passive people into activists and so every time every one of these things is...there is a process that you go through and without the goal, how do you know if you achieve success? You've got to have something to measure what your pursuit is.*

When did it first occur to him that he could be Governor and he set that as a goal?

In 1987 I was Secretary of Commerce and that was my first taste of Tallahassee, first taste of State Government and I saw the power for good, the potential for doing things, achieving things in the Office of the Governor, working for Governor Martinez. I saw his successes and I saw his missed opportunities and I kind of had a front row seat for a couple years watching how that worked. It really got me interested, not in a active way but in a passive way. I had a complication which was that my Dad was Vice President and then running for President and it was clear to me that it would be inappropriate for me to run for office while my Dad was in public light. So I kind of put it away and then in 1992, after he lost, I was actively involved in the campaign here. I made up my mind.

In setting a goal you have to **be reasonably specific.** "I want to be a success" will not cut it. "I want to be rich" is likewise too vague. "I want to be loved and admired by the masses", aside from other issues it raises, lacks the specificity required in effective goal setting. Much better to say "I want to make x dollars a year in three years," or "I want to be elected dog catcher in the 2006 local election." Having set a specific goal, you are then able to formulate and implement the plans to achieve it. The goal can be a relatively modest one (since, once you achieve it, you will immediately set a new goal. As **Senator Bob Graham** told me, *"If you've accomplished everything you want, then you haven't pushed yourself hard enough."*). Or it can be a grand, audacious goal. It is wonderful to dream, and **the biggest accomplishers are invariably the biggest dreamers.**

One success book I really like was not the best selling of the genre and is not yet considered among the classics. Written in 1991 and already containing some dated references, the book is *If it ain't broke...Break It* by performance coach Robert J. Kriegel and Dr. Louis Patler. In the book the authors talk about the importance of dreams and the pursuit of dreams. While researching for a book, Kriegel interviewed 500 top performers from all areas of work, arts and sports. He found that

> No two were alike, but the one quality they had in common was passion. It was their drive, their enthusiasm, their desire that distinguished them. They were passionate and excited about what they were doing.
>
> Passion: a burning commitment brings your whole being into play—body, mind, and spirit—making you feel more vital and fully alive and enabling you to tap inner strengths, resources, abilities and energies that you didn't know existed. Passion kindles a spark that inspires you and others around you to greater heights.

****

> Imagine how strong the passion and persistence of the great inventors, discoverers, and visionaries must have been, enabling them to avoid getting their ideas dampened or extinguished prematurely.

Wayne Huizenga told me the same thing:

You can't be all things to all people. You find something that you are passionate about and you work on that.

He went on to say:

We still have a passion for what we do. It's not making the investment for the sake of making the investment. It still is having fun. If you are enthused and excited about it, you work at it harder. And you get up in the morning and you're still thinking about what you should be doing and so forth.... Once in a while I come across something and I'll talk to the kids and they said nah, that's not for me, and I say I'm going to buy this anyway. So I buy it for my wife and me. I still enjoy. I'm not ready to retire yet.

Senator **Bob Graham** had a long and distinguished career. Only at the end of his Senate career, in 2004, did he decide to take a run for the Presidency. He felt for the first time that he was ready to undertake it and explained the factors. One of the most important considerations was that he felt the country was in a place where his children and grandchildren might be worse off than we are because of mistakes his country was making today. He told me,

*There was one other thing that was probably more important than all of the above and that was passion. My sister-in-law, Katherine Graham [late owner of the Washington Post] had known every President from Coolidge until her death, while George W. Bush was President. She said the one **thing that distinguished persons who run successfully for President and serve successfully as President was passion. They had to feel very deeply that what they were doing was important to transcend ego or personal ambition.** I frankly hadn't felt that passion until the experiences of the early part of this century.*

Novelist **Brad Meltzer** was also fortunate enough to find his passion:

*I'm not a self-hating lawyer, I won't say that, so I'm not like one of those people who says "oh, I just couldn't wait to get away from law school and I hated it and I was miserable". Actually I loved law school. I think the law and the concept is interesting. I think it's fascinating. I just think **you have to follow your passion and my passion is to write** and when I started doing it I just didn't know that. When I started law school and applied for law school I didn't know that I loved to write at that point. So I didn't go to law school because I wanted book ideas. I went to law school because I just didn't know what else I was going to do with my time, and I also knew that I had to pay off some college. I had grown up in a very normal environment, and I just felt that if everything goes to pot and this* *writing doesn't work out, I should have something to fall back on. So on that level it was my own cowardly choice. I wasn't going to wait tables and play the starving artist, because I knew what it was like to have money issues, and I didn't want to have those money issues. So that was why I went to law school. What happened there once I got there I never expected.*

Likewise, **Jorge de Cespedes**, President of PharMed and co-owner of the Charlotte Bobcats, recognizes how critical following your passion is to your success:

Absolutely, absolutely [passion is a big factor]. *You know, when you look at life realistically,* **most successful people probably spend 40 to 50% of their time, of their waking hours, around their business. If you don't like what you are doing and you can't have passion...I think that you should be happy in your life in what you are doing and the work place also. I constantly tell people: "listen I understand work is work and but you need to really get into what you are doing".** *Get whatever end of the business you want to get into—the financial end or the fact that you are somehow in the health care business to help people's lives, be healthier...whatever it is that motivates you. And I'm not suggesting 100% of our people are that way, but I am suggesting that most of our people....they feel the same. Certainly the nine that became millionaires in January felt that way. They have their passion and they were key people in helping us have the success and leading to it.*

That passion is a consistent theme among the super-successful. **Susan Story**, CEO of Gulf Power Co., explaining her passion for the electric utility business, practically sizzles with electric energy:

Every day I get up, I can't wait to come to work. I will tell you, probably one of the most rewarding experiences I have had in my two years as CEO of Gulf Power was one of the biggest catastrophes that hit this area, and that was Hurricane Ivan in September 2004. Where our area was devastated....We had a storm surge, we had high winds, there was no electricity; we had zero electricity. It was just devastating, and to be part of an effort that brought in people from 23 states and Canada to get the power back up to people within 13 days, when we really thought it would be 3 to 4 weeks, and to be part of just bringing the electricity back, but bringing hope back to the community that needed normalcy and needed routine. I consider the work I do to be critical to people's lives.... I do the work I do, and I had a choice when I came out of college to do almost anything I wanted to do. I could never work for a company that I did not think was doing something that made a difference for the better or the good of the community. I just couldn't. And I know what we do makes a difference in people's lives....

I will tell you a perfect story. We had 18 employees lose everything. They lost their homes. All they had was a slab left. 200 employees had major damage. They were all at work the day of the hurricane; the day it came they were all at work later that day. We had a reporter from Washington who I introduced to a young woman. I said, 'this is Kim McDaniel and she lost everything.' And it's the day following the storm. The reporter looked at her and said, 'If you lost everything, why are you here?" She looked him in the eye and said, 'because we've got to get the power back on.' That's why my job is a job. Because I work with people who say our job is bigger than coming here and producing and selling electricity. We're here to make people's lives better, and people depend on us, and regardless of my personal hardships, I'm going to do this because it makes a difference. That's why I love the work I do. And that's why I love the industry I'm in.

So, by all means, dream the dream. **Formulate a specific and grand goal.**

Then Do It!

Here is where we get to step two. To **dream without action is folly.** Nothing will ever come of setting your goal (unless you count enduring frustration) if you do not set about a plan of action to achieve it. It never ceases to amaze me how many people have big plans or dreams... and then spend all their time and mental energy nurturing the dream without ever taking practical steps to accomplish it. Dreams without action are a waste, and, the worst part is that people who live that way are inevitably disappointed and frustrated.

Bob Graham, former Governor of and U.S. Senator from Florida:

My feeling is to be really happy and to maximize your chances of being successful. You need to view each day as the most important day of your life, because it's the only day that you can substantially influence. So December 27, 2004 is the most important day and you need to pour everything that you can into that day, not feel that you've got to hold back or something is going to happen a week a month, a year or more.

*And you don't **get diverted by dreaming about the future**. Now, I'm not saying that you shouldn't have some general goals. You ought to have an idea of what you'd like to be doing, but the way you get there is not just by focusing on your goal. It's to make each day as contributory to achieving that goal.*

*They are both important and they interact with each other. **What you want to avoid is by saying, well I've set a goal, I want to be the best trial lawyer in the State of Florida, and then not taking the actions day by day that would build a foundation to actually be the best trial lawyer** in the State of Florida.*

Jorge de Cespedes, President of PharMed:

Ok, you have to have passion. You have to go forward with a plan, knowing that you are going to have obstacles. You can't quit; you've got to move forward, knowing that tomorrow is another day. OK and last but not least, you have execution and this is where a lot people don't do it. I'm sure in your field as an attorney, as well as any field, you have a lot of people with vision, who really want to make it, but they can't execute.

When I was in law school I had an interest in politics. I thought I would like to be elected to public office to affect public policy (or, in the do-gooder lingo of the young, to make the world a better place for the average citizen). The trouble was, I had very little idea how to go about doing it and recognized that the practical aspects of politics (detailed organization, public speaking, approaching strangers with an outgoing self-confident air) were not really my strong suits. At the time

I was in law school I knew a number of my fellow law students who had the same desires. Not only did they want to run for and hold public office, they had spent their youth preparing. They had studied politics, worked for politicians, held office in statewide and national Democrat or Republican Clubs. Their egos allowed them to boast that they would be future Governors or Senators. I moved to Florida for law school when I was 20. I did not have any of the contacts these other people had. In fact, I knew no one in Florida. I graduated from law school at the age of 23. At the age of 26 I was elected to the Florida House of Representatives and served three terms in the Legislature.

None of the law school classmates who were destined for big things in politics was ever elected to office. Why was I able to achieve that goal and these other people, some undoubtedly better suited for the quest, were not? In my opinion it was because the minute I decided to set that goal, I spent no more energy convincing myself I can or I should. I did. And I certainly did not waste energy reminding myself of all the obstacles or why it was going to be difficult or impossible. I methodically set about a plan to achieve the goal. It included educating myself about the State and its issues, selecting the right constituency, selecting the appropriate party affiliation, finding issues that I could make my own, meeting the people I had to know, and winning over those whose help I would need. When the time came to run I was prepared. That is when the hard work began. Holding yourself up as "available" to be elected rarely gets anyone a majority of votes. It is grueling, sweaty work. Not just finding the right theme, but also spending whatever hours it takes to walk door to door (or in the case of Miami Beach, poolside to poolside, card room to card room). If you have never spent several hours a day in July, August and September in Miami, Florida, walking in a business suit at the side of teeming swimming pools, bending over to smile and chat at every opportunity while the sweat is running down your back, you may have trouble understanding the level of commitment that is necessary in taking the **actions you must take to achieve your goal**.

So what distinguished me from all those other would-be Governors and Senators? It is quite simple. **They dreamed it. I did it**. For all their aspirations, they never ran for office. Why not? Perhaps the same egos that caused them to picture themselves as office holders would not let them overcome the potential ignominy of defeat. If you stop to think about the prospect of losing, it may deter you from entering the race. **There is only one sure way not to lose: not to try.**

How much agonizing did **Jeb Bush** give to his goal to become Governor, once he had set that goal? Not very much:

> *I didn't think about it too hard. I'm not big on sitting on a couch and reflecting.* **I think a lot of times people stumble over their doubts. It's not appropriate to be rash, but it's equally not appropriate to fret. It feels right and its right. Get comfortable with the decision; you have to pull the trigger and move on.**

I can confidently assure you that when you are older and look back on opportunities you had, *you will have far fewer regrets for that which you tried and failed than for that which you failed to try.* What distinguished me from the rest of this crowd of would-be-Presidents was really pretty simple. I ran for office, and they did not. I did not let fear of losing deter me from entering the game.

Nike is not so far off the mark with their slogan: Just Do It!! Donald Trump says "People agonize over details for months and nothing ever happens." **Things happen for the doers.**

I applied the same principle when it came to becoming a lawyer, and, more important, the type of lawyer I wanted to be. By the time I moved from New York to start law school in Miami, I had read the local papers and determined there were two lawyers I wanted to meet and learn from. One was a man who was the leading advocate for civil rights, human rights, First Amendment. He handled all the high profile American Civil Liberties Union (ACLU) cases of the 60's. The other was a man who knew better than anyone how to get and win cases for the underdog—be it a civil case against a big corporation, or a criminal case where the individual was facing the awesome power of the State—and he knew how to get his name in the papers doing it. By the time I had finished law school I was interning for both men, neither of whom I had ever met before moving to Florida. I simply planned to meet them and let them know that I admired their work, and wanted to work with them and learn from them. And so I did. For the crusading ACLU lawyer I had the privilege to write important appellate briefs advocating major Constitutional positions, and for the notorious (he was well-known, but not always well-liked) champion of the underdog, I got to assist in preparation of some very high profile trials.

I have another example from the same period of my life. When I decided to move to Miami, I did do some research about the community. I learned that there was then living in Miami a retired two term United States Senator from the State of Washington. He was a prominent civic leader in Miami. I placed a cold call to him (probably more than one until I got through). I told him I was in law school, that I was interested in politics, that I admired his career and I was wondering if he could spare a few minutes to meet with me. He said, yes, and I went to his office. Over the next few months we met several times and I got to pick his brain for advice that it would not have been possible to find in a book or to pay for. I learned that if you **ask accomplished people for advice and guidance**, they are often very happy to share their knowledge and experience with you.

As a novelist, **Brad Meltzer**, often has to rely on people to help.

I'm a firm believer that [people want to help you]. *You know, some people call me naïve, some people call me an optimist, but I'm a firm believer of that. I make my living trying to get into government buildings and to sneak into government-guarded structures and find out how the government works. I write thrillers about the White House and the Supreme Court and Congress and people will say, "well, how do you get inside" and I always said, "I ask," and I say if someone calls you tomorrow and they said, "listen I'm writing a book on your occupation, I need a half hour of your time just talking about what your job is like, would you mind sparing a half hour?" Ninety-nine percent of the people will say yes. Why? Because people are generally nice. They want to help you and they said ah, that's cool, you're writing a book, let me help you out, and I rely a lot on the kindness of those strangers. I feel like given half a chance, people will be encouraging.*

My older daughter, too, has a story that shows the importance of setting a goal and then doing what it takes to make it reality. As she was on a dual law and psychology track, she called me one day to say that she had convinced a professor to allow her to do independent study on jury selection. She asked if I knew any jury consultant with whom she could intern. I did not, but I asked the prominent criminal attorney, Roy Black. He told me whom he used and volunteered to introduce Marni to his consultant and also suggested she could work with both of them on a big murder case they were beginning. Marni interned for that gentleman during her senior year at law school. After law school she met Amy Singer, probably one of the most preeminent trial consultants in the country. The two got along well and Amy mentored her. By the time she was just 30 years old, Marni had become one of the best thought-of trial consultants in Florida. You can check out her web site at www.TheRightJury.com. She loves her work and does it well. All because, having found her goal, she then acted on it.

What if you have no clear idea of what you like and no burning passion you can identify? It is startling how many young people reach the end of college, or even the years after college, without having identified something that they can passionately embrace as a career goal. For those people, my advice is to experiment and experience as many different options as possible. If you graduate college, you may feel compelled (by guilt or financial necessity or peer/parent pressure) to start working at something. Anything. I think that is a mistake. It would not be a waste of two months if you were to spend one day for each of fifty working days "testing the waters."

By this I mean you should experience as many of the occupations or professions as you can imagine. I do not mean spending a year or two at a variety of different jobs. When I get a resume from someone who has had four jobs in five years, I don't even bother going further. There may be a good story which would explain such instability, but I am not interested in spending my time hearing the stories and discerning the truth. What I am referring to is a quick "taste tour." You could spend one day with a lawyer, one day with a stockbroker, one day with a restaurant chef; spend a day with a realtor, with a teacher, with a professional musician (if you can play something requiring more talent than a kazoo). Spend a day with a doctor or nurse, with a journalist, with an accountant or a Human Resource Director. You get the idea. I could continue listing professions or occupations for pages and not run out. So could you. So do so. Pick some obvious one and some that are way out (taxidermist?). Then do some research and find the good ones, those with an excellent reputation in your area. Call them. Tell them you are graduating or have graduated from college and you think you might like to be a....whatever it is they do, but you are not sure. You would like to spend one day with him or her just observing, to be his or her shadow. You would be amazed that most would be pleased with your interest and delighted to help in this way.

Clarence Otis, CEO of Darden Restaurants, sought the counsel of other people in trying to make career decisions:

> *I talked to quite a few people and one of the guys—a lot of them were sort of part of the Williams* [the College he went to] *network, you know the Williams Alumni network. It's pretty close. If you call on people, they'll be with you, they'll sit down and talk. Williams has a pretty good presence on Wall Street. I talked to a fellow named Foster Devereau, whose is a partner at Allen & Company, which is a boutique investment bank in New York. I talked to another guy I knew at Merrill Lynch, and then I knew a classmate who was at Kidder Peabody, which is where I joined.*

> *People sure are* [willing to help]. *It is interesting. Because people will share their knowledge with you and give you their point of view, and that was very helpful going through that process.*

Recently I met and interviewed a young lawyer. Before law school she had graduated from college and had a decent career in marketing. One day she was visiting a friend who is a judge and spent a day just sitting in the judge's courtroom. She was fascinated, and knew right away that this was what she wanted to do. So she did. She went to Law School and became a lawyer. It is interesting how many people end up in careers that are not those they set out to enter, and may not even be related to the college curriculum they originally pursued.

My youngest brother-in-law is a good example. He graduated from college with a degree, by default, in finance. He had no particular reason for choosing that major other than the explanation Sir Edmund Hillary gave for being the first to climb Mt. Everest: it was there. After graduation, he took a dead-end job answering phones in an accounting firm. Then, to make more money, he took an even more dead-end job selling dental supplies. How do you suppose he felt every day when he woke up for work? Yet, he had an unexplored natural talent. If my wife or I or any family member had a stiff neck or aching back, he would be able to massage it out, instinctively finding the right spot and applying the right pressure. He was a natural healer and he loved helping people. We suggested he go back to school and become a physical therapist.

Changing careers so radically was not easy. Already married, he and his wife had to make a financial sacrifice so he could go back to college. Since he had no science prerequisites, it was almost two years more of undergraduate work before he could take the necessary graduate curriculum. But he stuck with it, and before age 30 found himself doing something that he really enjoys, and something he is really good at, making a difference for the people he treats and their families.

Getting to the point of taking action is not always easy. You do have to take risks. **Rarely is anything worth accomplishing undertaken without risk.** This does not mean crazy or potentially fatal risks (unless your goal is to be a great test pilot), but you cannot be afraid to take risks that others walk away from. (If your goal is indeed to be a great test pilot or race car driver, I am reminded of a line in an old movie starring James Garner, *Grand Prix*, in which one character explains that in order to be a great race driver "You have to have a certain lack of imagination.") I once met U.S. Senator John Glenn who had been the first man to orbit the earth in a space capsule. When he had made his historic flight, his heart rate reportedly had gone up only one beat a minute. I asked how he could be so cool under pressure, and he, too, jokingly cited lack of imagination.

It is important that once you have set your goal and are committed to action, that you **recognize the difference between activity (undirected) and action (clearly directed).** Activity can be an unfocused expenditure of energy; you may be talking about your goal, thinking about it, and randomly doing things that skirt around the necessary things you must do to reach the goal. Action is far more focused and involves doing. Not only doing, but doing those things that systematically advance the plan you have laid out to succeed. You should have a "to do" list of those things you must act on to advance your objective.

The trouble I have found with many people, even those who are aware of the value of "to do" lists, is that they jump around on the list, usually dispensing with the easy tasks first. Not surprisingly, the important tasks linger from day to day. There is lots of activity, but not the necessary action. The best advice I can offer on the subject of **setting priorities and taking action** is this: When you make your "to do" list, list them in the order of priority, the most important and the most difficult tasks first. Then attack them in order, checking each off as it is done. (For a whole book devoted to the best use of your time, see Peter Drucker's *The Effective Executive*.) If you skip around the list, doing the easy tasks first, you can deceive yourself into believing you are just getting the simple things out of the way so you will have more time for the important ones. However, you never do seem to get to the important ones, and, as author and motivational speaker Brian Tracy says, you get into the habit of doing unimportant things. (Many psychologists would suggest that this unproductive behavior is the way some people deliberately undermine themselves, assuring they do not reach their goals, perhaps out of fear of trying, or even fear of success.) Better to **develop the habit of tackling the important things first and moving ever closer to your goals**.

So, when I was contemplating a life in politics, how did I muster up the courage to walk up to strangers in every restaurant and every street corner and introduce myself and ask for their vote? Easy, you might say, if you are an outgoing person. But I grew up pretty quiet and shy. To reach the goal I set for myself, I had to be ready and willing to change my very nature, to do things that did not come naturally. That was the first action step. I owe my ability to do so to Richard (Dick) Stone. Dick Stone was a young lawyer in Miami when I was in law school. He was running (successfully) for the State Senate, and later became Florida's Secretary of State, then a United States Senator, and later the U.S. Ambassador to Denmark. When I first met him, I was a law student at University of Miami. One evening I was attending a Young Democrats party with a couple of friends. As was normally the case, we were sitting pretty much by ourselves, not really mingling or engaging others at the party. Along came a young man, walked up to us, held out his hand and said, "Hi, I'm Dick Stone, and I'm running for State Senate. I hope you will support me."

At that moment I had an epiphany: I realized, unlike many other politicians I had met, that this did not come easily to him. In fact, I thought he had to work very hard to force himself to come over to us and introduce himself, but there was no question that he was doing what he had to do and would continue to do so. That very moment, the thought crossed my mind: "If he can do that, so can I," and that was the moment I knew I would run for office and have no trouble doing what it would take. It was simply **acting out a role**. (There is something else I owe Dick Stone. Years later when he was a U.S. Senator and I was visiting him in Washington, D.C., he took my wife and me to lunch at a Japanese restaurant and introduced us to Sushi. It was the first time I tried Sushi, and it has been a part of our culinary experiences ever since.)

I mentioned that in going around shaking hands with strangers, asking them to vote for me, I approached it as though I was playing a role. That is one way to do something that might seem difficult in the moment. My younger daughter was a theater major and already quite a good actress. I remember when she was 16, the first month she had a car. She had driven some friends to visit a music recording studio in the next county. As she was driving on the highway, a car sideswiped her, pulled directly in front of her and stopped short. She reacted quickly but still tapped the car in front of her. (This is actually an old insurance scam, where people make a living by forcing rear end collisions.) She called me from the road, obviously very upset. I told her to calm down. I said that soon the police would arrive and how they would handle the situation would depend on her demeanor. I said that she is sure to be in trouble if they see a hysterical child. I said that she would be fine if they saw a poised young woman. She took a deep breath and said, "Poised young woman. I can play that." And so she did. She took out her always-handy camera, photographed the scene from all sides, the uninjured people in the other car, and when the police arrived they sent her on her way with no ticket. She had successfully played the role in which she was cast. It is not a bad way to undertake difficult situations that may confront you.

The bottom line to rounding out the two steps to success is that having set your goal, **go for it**. Yes, it is true that often life gets in the way. There are jobs to do because we have to eat, and kids to raise and support. You may feel you do not have the time to commit to give it 100%. These are convenient excuses but only excuses. It is simply a matter of making the goal a priority. You can just give up, or you can get yourself into the game. Once you enter the game, play to win. Sitting around thinking about what you want, what might be, what could have been...is a losing game. Take all the time you need to formulate a meaningful goal. Then determine the necessary steps to reach it, and finally, distinguishing yourself from the crowd, do it.

REFLECTIONS AND APPLICATION—CHAPTER 4

1. List two goals you have had in the past but did <u>not</u> achieve.
2. For each, what action should you have taken to advance the goal but failed to take or complete?
3. For each action you failed to take or complete, write down the reason or rationalization you gave yourself for not doing it.
4. For each such rationalization, what response can you offer today to overcome the reason for or objection to taking action?
5. If the goal is still one that you would aspire to, then what action step is necessary NOW to advance toward it? Commit to taking that step this week, and DO IT. No excuses, please.
6. Make a list of what interests you (it can be a thing like "rocks", an activity like "music" or "surfing", a bird or dog, children, a car—anything at all, or several things). For each then do research on all the careers that involve or touch upon that activity or thing. If you do it right, you will come up with a pretty long list.
7. Make a list of activities or talents about which you are passionate or better than most people you know (sleeping and day dreaming do not count unless you want to be a psychologist or night watchman). Again, research all the careers that involve or touch upon that activity or talent.
8. Set a goal that you want to accomplish, (a) this month, (b) within a year, (c) within 5 years. Visualize the goal accomplished. What will you look like? How will it feel?
9. Now write out the specific steps you must take to achieve the goals, most important ones first. Is there a person you must call for advice? Make the call. A course you must take? Register now.

CHAPTER 5
THE SECOND SECRET: KNOWING YOUR LIMITATIONS

This is a trick Chapter heading because the real rule is this: **You have no limitations except the ones you put on yourself.** It is just too long for the title of a chapter. If you accept that there are limitations on what you can achieve then you have built in that reality. If you understand and believe that there are no limitations, then you have created the conditions for a far better alternative reality.

But, you will say, are there not natural laws, physical limitations, things "everyone knows" that limit what we can accomplish? Well, if you are 140 pounds, it is reasonably certain you are not going to be an NFL linebacker, but within reasonable bounds, **if you can think it and you believe it, you can do it.**

As schoolchildren we have probably all heard and even memorized the poem by 19th century English poet William Ernest Henly. The first and last stanzas are these:

> OUT of the night that covers me,
> Black as the Pit from pole to pole,
> I thank whatever gods may be
> For my unconquerable soul.
>
> It matters not how strait the gate,
> How charged with punishments the scroll,
> I am the master of my fate:
> I am the captain of my soul.

We read it, we know it, but do we fully accept it? Do we really believe that we are the masters of our fates? We should, because more than anything else, that belief is what will determine success.

During the 1992 Presidential election, I remember watching an interview of third party Independent candidate, Ross Perot. Perot is a self made billionaire who ran for President and undoubtedly had an impact on framing the debate of the issues, and possibly the outcome. An interviewer asked him this:

"Mr. Perot, you have been so successful in business, yet so many people who start a business fail. How do you explain the difference?"

"I have found," Perot said, "that successful people just don't know when they have failed."

In other words, against all contrary evidence, successful people **envision a successful outcome** to what they are doing. They believe in what they are doing and that they will achieve their goals. They then follow through with their belief and keep on going, often against all odds or rational evidence. Marconi, the inventor of the radio, was sent to a mental hospital because he believed he could send messages through the air. There are more modern examples. In his autobiography, Henry Ford explains that he quit his job and went into the car business even though everyone told him that there was no mass market for the low cost automobiles he wanted to produce. Michael Dell, in his autobiography, relates how most knowledgeable people told him it would be impossible to compete with companies like IBM; that his idea of direct selling of computers to the public (bypassing traditional distribution channels) on a mass basis could never work.

Evidently all the smart people were wrong, and Ford and Dell who believed in their ideas and in themselves became very rich. Moreover, they had a major impact on the world. Imagine the difference between a world in which a few wealthy people have hobby cars and one in which every household has at least one car, and often several. Imagine the difference between a world in which only businesses and wealthy individuals have personal computers versus one in which 80% of the households in the country have a PC and access to the Internet. The difference between those worlds stems from the belief of those two individuals in what they could do, notwithstanding the common knowledge of their times. Just as you must if you want to succeed, these men believed in themselves and were strong enough to keep on going and prove everyone else wrong. They did not let the nay-sayers get to them, and neither should you.

Another good example of this is Fred Smith. You may not have heard of him but you certainly have heard of the company he founded, Federal Express. He came up with the idea for Federal Express as a project for a Harvard Business School paper. Unfortunately, Mr. Smith only got a grade of C minus. His professor felt the business plan was flawed and it would never work as a business. Fortunately for those who absolutely positively have to get it there overnight, Mr. Smith listened to himself and not to the expert. He had his dream and he pursued it. As a result, the world is a lot smaller today and Mr. Smith is a lot richer.

If you have an idea you want to pursue, a dream you want to live, then the best advice I can give is: **Go for it**. If you want to approach a successful and well known person in the field you want to have a career in, and ask that person for advice, why would you not do so? What is the worst you could hear? "No." OK, you are then no worse off than before you asked. Go on and ask your next choice. If you want a position that requires a test, do not let your fears and doubts deter you from preparing for and taking the test. What is the worst that could happen? You would not pass it. You would not be worse off than you had been before. In fact, you would be better off because you now would have experience in taking the test and could take it next time a little more relaxed and a little more confident. The point is, we all sometimes let our fears deter us from reaching for the brass ring. **Put aside the fears**. Bravery is not the absence of fear. It is doing what we have to do in spite of the fear. If we fall short of achieving our dreams, too often it is because we did not dare to reach for them. We let our doubts creep up and take over. We imposed limitations on ourselves and lived down to them.

When I was in law school, I encountered an early example of how we let fears and doubts deter us. Confronting those fears actually altered the course of my law school career, and perhaps even the course of my professional life. It was second semester of the first year, and I was in a course on Civil Procedure (the procedures used to navigate the court process in non-criminal cases). The Professor was Minnette Massey. She had been a Dean of the Law School and teaching law at University of Miami for 20 years at that time. (She retired after teaching the same subject to my daughter Marni 30 years later—I don't think that accounted for her retirement, it was just coincidental.) Professor Massey was a tough lady, austere and serious. Students feared her and would wither under her barbed questioning in class. It was truly the real life version of the law professor in the movie, *The Paper Chase* (which everyone contemplating law school should see).

At that time I generally preferred sitting quietly in class, never raising my hand to answer a question, and hoping never to be called on. In Miss Massey's class I think I deliberately sat in the most inconspicuous location in the lecture hall and sat even lower in the seat. She would pace the front, and when she was ready to call on the next victim, would study the seating chart. She would look at the chart, then at the student sitting in the corresponding location. Look at the chart and back to the student. And finally, call out the name: "Mr. Becker." The name would hit the poor student like a punch to the stomach, and the question and answer to follow were usually more painful.

One day a few of us law students were studying a civil procedure assignment in the library. We came upon an issue to which none of us knew the answer. After some back and forth debate, I suggested: "we can ask Miss Massey." Everyone agreed that that was better than the alternative of not learning the answer and looking even more foolish in class, so we marched down the hall to her office and stood in front of the door. Then, we debated who would knock and lead us in. The others said it had been my idea so I should do it. After some initial resistance, I relented and timidly knocked on her door, desperately hoping she was not in and I would escape to live another day. But it was not to be. We heard, "Come in."

I opened the door slowly and stuck in only my head. Professor Massey looked up from her desk. Then a big smile crossed her face and she said, "Alan! Come on in!" In that moment I realized it had all been a game. She didn't need that name chart. She knew her students and really cared about them. A wave of relaxation passed through me and I was never the same in her class or any other.

After that incident, she would call on me more often. Emboldened now with the knowledge that her classroom demeanor was a show, I would often answer with a wisecrack (generally accompanied by the correct answer, which helps) or a double entendre. The first time I tried it, the other students audibly gasped. But Professor Massey would return in kind, and it seemed at times that we had a dialogue going that we were the only two people in the midst of the large lecture class who got it. One day a couple of classmates said to me that I should not be speaking in class the way I was, that it would anger the Professor. So I sought her out and asked, Professor, does the way I answer in class upset you? She said, "Alan, it keeps me up all night." I had my answer and my green light. The green light to be myself, to enjoy law school, and to never again let fear or doubt guide my decisions about school or life. I am sure I have told her this in person many years later, but for the record, Thank you, Professor Massey. (Oh, and I also learned Civil Procedure.)

In an interview discussing her amazing show business comeback, comedian Ellen DeGeneres said: "I was raised with a lot of fear, and I witnessed people who never did anything out of the what-ifs and the fears. I didn't want to end up that way." In other words, she made a choice not to let fears govern her actions.

We all know what she means by "the what-ifs". I want to make a trip, but what if I can't get an affordable ticket; and if I do, what if I don't get to the airport on time; and if I do, what if I am stopped at security; and if I get through security, what if I am too tired to lug my bags to the plane; and if I get on the plane, what if there are sick people on it and I catch cold; and if I don't catch cold, what if the plane crashes; and if it doesn't crash, what if it arrives late and I miss my connection...." You get the idea. I could go on with the one example for pages more, but I will spare you. You can compound all the things that can go wrong in any scenario. Imagine how many things there are for a show business person to fear, from lack of bookings to lack of audience reaction. So most people are defeated before they begin because the "what-ifs" take hold and deter them from moving forward. They fall prey to the disease of "what-can-go-wrong-itis" and dwell on the things that can go wrong, rather than on the things that can go right.

Frankly, it is exhausting to imagine all those things that can go wrong, and usually **we imagine things a lot worse than the reality we will find**. Winston Churchill, reflecting on this tendency, said: "When I look back on all these worries I remember the story of the old man who said on his deathbed that he had had a lot of trouble in his life, most of which never happened." Far better to imagine all the positive things that can unfold and **maintain focus on the positive**.

Needless to say, any successful person must take one step at a time, and even if something bad does happen, they push on past it. They certainly do not dwell on it or let the fear of it consume their thoughts.

In fact, there is a positive side to what-ifs. Try imagining the opposite: what if I get on the plane and have a pleasant flight and arrive at a great location on time and have a wonderful time. What if I keep auditioning and I find the perfect role and I get cast, and the audience loves me, and I get great reviews. **Positive visualization** can be as powerful in propelling you forward as negative visualization can be in holding you back. **Strive always to have a positive attitude,** as that is a common denominator of successful people. As Wayne Dyer, whom I consider an important inspirational contemporary philosopher, says, "Contemplate yourself as surrounded by the conditions you wish to produce." **Positive attitude and positive visualization are essential** to get you where you want to be.

Visualization is an important aide to achieve success. Picture yourself as a captain of industry, or receiving that big pay check. Actor Jim Carey, who now gets $20 million dollars a movie, was once struggling and living in his car. He carried in his wallet a check made payable to him for $20 million for his work on a movie. He had written it to himself as a constant reminder of what he wanted to achieve. Would the day have come without that reminder? Maybe, but he believes having it was a big help, and I think he is right. Athletes often visualize themselves winning—be it crossing the finish line first, or sinking the basket or "seeing" the golf ball go into the hole. See yourself holding the trophy and accepting the adulation of your peers, and the vision will accelerate the journey to the reality.

Jorge de Cespedes, President of PharMed, told me the same thing:

> *It takes the same amount of time and energy to be average as to be great. It really does. It's how you go about it, it's how you're visualizing. I give motivational talks, and I talk about these things. First you have to have a vision. You actually have to visualize yourself where you want to be, whether it's on 100 foot yacht or in your country house in the northeast. You have to visualize that ok so you have to have vision.*

If there is something you want to achieve, when is the best time to begin the effort? The answer is unequivocally, NOW! You can always think of reasons to delay. **Procrastination is the enemy of accomplishment.** It is the manifestation of those limitations we put on ourselves. We do it in the little things of every day life and it becomes a habit of self defeat. Should I clean the living room now or play a music video. The video is more fun, so the cleaning waits. Should I write the report due next week now, or should I watch a program on TV. We can all convince ourselves that we are tired now and deserve that hour to relax, and besides, the report is not due until next week. There is plenty of time to do the less pleasant things that must be done. Wrong! **The time to do what you have to do is NOW.** The time to do what you fear but know you should do is NOW. Get it out of the way now, and move on to the next important step. Because NOW thinking is so critical to success, I have always referred to it as "The Power of Now."[7] You can dream and plan forever, but you will not have a chance at success until you begin taking action, and the time to take action is NOW. **Now thinking is the energy that will empower your dreams and propel them toward reality.**

Another enemy of "Now Thinking" and another form of procrastination is "perfection". My younger daughter was one of these people. In high school she would often have to do a report. She would agonize over it, work hard on it, even starting well before it was due. Yet when the time came for the report to be turned in, she was not finished. Why? Because it was never perfect enough. Well, I have news for you: few things in life are perfect. **Finished is better than perfect.** I think I have finally convinced her that 95% of perfect and finished on time is better than the self-sabotage of never believing what you do is good enough. In most things, *good enough is not good enough,* but when you let an irrational quest for perfection take hold and deter forward motion, then you are creating a barrier to your own success.

A book I found in England has a remarkably understated title. It is simply, *Success,* by Richard Hall. It has many references to people and history that will be unfamiliar to the American reader, but a message that works anywhere. Hall combines the two thoughts in the prior paragraph when he says:

> So the next time anyone tells you (this, by the way, is constantly being told to me) they are not a good completer/finisher, do me a favour and consider punching them really hard as you cry, 'it's not a bleeding university—*just do it will you?*'—WHACK....

> If you can't complete or execute you don't really deserve
> to be in employment. True success lies in execution.
> *True success lies in results.*
> Much of this book has an 'up and at 'em' flavour. But
> the essence of being a great doer isn't about random
> action: it's absolutely about having a clear plan and
> then performing it—brilliantly.

Sounds, in a British way, an awful lot like: Set a goal. Do it. Finish.

It is amazing how our own perceptions of who we are or what we can do can make or break us. Too often, we heap limitations on our own selves that are unjustified and inhibit our forward progress in life. I remember seeing a movie in 1983, *All the Right Moves*, with Tom Cruise. Cruise plays a young high school athlete in a dying Pennsylvania steel town. He is desperate to win a football scholarship, so he would be able to go to college. As he saw it, that was his only way to escape the fate of his father and brother who stayed in the town and worked for the steel mill. Without the football scholarship, he constantly moaned, his vision of freedom would be doomed and with its demise he would be condemned to life in the mill. In the end, he clashed with his coach and it cost him his scholarship. Woe is me. This was the end of a potentially productive life. I walked out of the movie just shaking my head.

I simply could not understand people who accept their limitations without the brains or guts to fight back. Of course there was another way out of town. I asked my wife, "Hasn't he ever heard of a bus ticket?" It really can be that simple, but if you accept what history or "friends" or relatives convince you are the limitations on where you can go, what you can do, what you can accomplish—it is over. If, on the other hand, you march to your own drummer, you confidently take the risk to dream your dreams and go for them—or in the opening words of *Star Trek*, bravely go where no man has been before, then the odds suddenly and miraculously shift to your side.

What in the world was that boy in *All the Right Moves* thinking? If he wanted to get out of the steel town and build a better life, a ten dollar bus ticket would have gotten him to New York City, Philadelphia, Baltimore, or Washington, D.C. He was interested in sports, so he could have walked into every Sports Authority or Foot Locker or sports related store of any kind until he found a job. He could have stayed at the YMCA until he had that job and found a roommate, then gotten a small apartment. He could have signed up for one or two courses at night at the Community College, applying for student financial aid if it was necessary. He could have gotten a degree, found a career, and built a life.... If he had believed he could do it.... If anyone had ever told him he could do it.... if he had set a goal, and if he had then done it. Instead he was limited by the limitations he had imposed on himself.

I truly believe that **there are no more powerful words than "Yes, I can."** (That is the title of singer Sammy Davis Jr.'s autobiography.) Success starts with belief that you can. And it can start very early if, as a toddler, you read *The Little Train that Could*. It is nurtured by the vision of what you want to achieve, i.e., you should **deliberately and repeatedly picture yourself having achieved the goal** you have set for yourself. You can visualize yourself doing something that you must accomplish in the next five minutes, just as a golfer will stand for a moment and mentally picture the ball following its predetermined course and going into the hole. Or, you can **visualize the outcome you want to achieve** in five years, such as the publisher of your yet-to-be-written book handing you a check for a $100,000 advance. Visualize it and then do so again and again. And believe in that vision and believe in yourself.

My younger daughter, Ilana, has set her sights upon success in one of the most competitive and difficult of professions: acting. Everyone will tell her that it is therefore important that she learn other skills so that she will have something to fall back on. Her response is always something that she says she first learned from her father (which is probably the case). She says: "If you have something to fall back on, you will fall back!" In other words, the very act of mentally setting a plan for what you will do when you fail at your goal, is the surest way to accept failure and in turn, to fail. The armies that fought most bravely, as they advanced, were the ones that burned the bridges behind them. There is no viable alternative to success.

REFLECTIONS AND APPLICATION—CHAPTER 5

1. Is there something that you are afraid of that stands in the way of your taking the steps to achieve your goal (e.g., fear of speaking in public, fear of rejection, fear of flying)? If you must, seek professional counseling. The best way to deal with the fear is not to try to make it go away but to do what you have to do despite it. Get up and speak (try a friendly audience first); walk up to strangers and ask for a dollar. Tell them you need to do this to get over your fear of rejection. You will get a lot of rejection and a lot of dollars. In spite of your fear of flying, force yourself onto an airplane, starting with a short flight.

2. If you do not use a "to do" list, make one now. Start with things you must do tomorrow. Keep it simple (buy groceries, do homework, call parents, make a date for Saturday). List the most important first. Then, putting aside all the reasons to delay (many will surface and you can convince yourself they are quite logical, if you let them intrude), do those things in the order you wrote them and check them off as they are completed. That night (and the next and the next), make the list for the next day. Keep repeating the exercise.

3. Have you any goals that you set aside because other people told you they were impossible or impractical? If so, write down the goal and the major objection. Now, write down two reasons you believe the goal is possible, and two counter arguments to the major objections.

(By the way, these "assignments" are not frivolous. They help develop the discipline necessary for success.)

CHAPTER 6
THE THIRD SECRET: GO WITH YOUR GUT

Every day we face choices. Some are pretty mundane: Should I have a cup of coffee now or will it affect my sleep tonight? Should I have a slice of that nice looking cake or will it just continue my cycle of gaining weight and loathing my lack of will power? Should I go up route 1 or take the Interstate to get where I am going more quickly? Of course, there are much bigger, life altering decisions. Should I go to the big University in the Northeast where it is colder, more competitive, with a reputation for turning out great engineers; or the smaller southern college that has a wonderful arts programs and an easier lifestyle? Should I marry this person who is a wonderful person that I get along well with, even though we do not have great romantic chemistry? Or this person with whom I have white hot attraction to and lust after, but is not my intellectual equal? Do I become an architect because my parents think I should, or pursue the far more speculative career as a rock guitarist?

It is true that some of those questions are susceptible to logical analysis. The little ones, such as which route to take, can be analyzed by traffic patterns and test runs. The big ones like which career to choose or who to marry also lend themselves to cold analysis. You could determine the salaries in different fields, the number of people unemployed, the number of businesses in that field in the area in which you want to live. You can make two lists to compare your potential life companion, listing good traits on one side, and negative ones on the other, and marry that person if your list ends up with more items in the plus column. My father-in-law actually did break his addiction to tobacco with two lists, i.e., the benefits of smoking vs. the harmful effects of smoking. Unfortunately, most people lack both the logic and discipline of my father-in-law.

Of course it does not really work this way. Yet, too often, we try to apply analytical processes to force a result when there is a much better way to figure out what you should be doing. What is that way? It is simply what I call going with your gut. In other words, when we make decisions, there are a lot of factors at play. Some we pragmatically investigate and analyze; some we instinctively know are correct. I believe that the instinctive decisions, the products of your intuition, are the best ones. **When we think too much about a decision we often will talk ourselves out of the right answer.** As **Jeb Bush**, Governor of Florida, told me in our interview: *"One of the things that I have learned in this job is that you can over process information."* How does Billionaire **Wayne Huizenga** decide whether to acquire a new business? *"The instinct comes first and the analysis comes later...."* And along the same lines, **Clarence Otis**, CEO of Darden Restaurants, explained his decision making process to me:

> I would say **there is a great deal of instinctive, and then you do analysis just to see if that instinct is the right instinct or not. But there is a pretty good feel, "yeah, this sort of fits me" as I know myself. So I'd say instinct is a significant percentage of it.**

We hear the same thing from **Susan Story**, CEO of Gulf Power Co.:

> Alan, I think a lot of what we do, **I have learned to trust my instinct more and more. Now I do think you have to couple instinct with experiential information and knowledge,** but through the experiences there are a lot of things that the facts tell me one thing, but I just know instinctually what the right thing to do is. **99% of the time, if not 100% of the time, what will unfold will show me that my instinct was right on target and I've learned that I really need to trust it because it's almost the second voice,** the second knowledge that we have that says this is the path you need to take.
>
> I think **it's interesting when we talk about when we're ready for changes in our careers or our lives, and people worry and they struggle with it. The one thing I found is, I just know when the time is right** and I've gotten to where I don't worry about that because I know when I get to the point that the decision is made and I have peace about it, that it just happens. And every time it does. For example, should you take this job, should you not? Should I retire now, should I not? When you look at it and you struggle with it, then one day you wake up and you say this is it, and you're at total

*peace and you know it's the right thing. I find that happens more and
more.*

I asked if Susan believes that sometimes people use too much logic to
talk themselves out of the right decision?

*Absolutely. And I can tell you with decisions that I make in my career
now, sometimes we go through the facts, and the facts clearly indicate
we need to take one path. But whenever I have this gnawing feeling
that says "I just don't know about this, I just don't know about this,"
I am learning to rely on that more. I have found that, almost always,
that is the correct path, but I had to learn through hard knocks.*

I think there is such a thing as too much logic. Too much logic
would have told Marconi that he should abandon the idea of the radio.
Too much logic would have deterred Christopher Columbus from betting
his life and a lot of other lives on the belief that they could cross an
uncharted ocean and find a new world. Too much logic would have
told Michael Dell to stay in college and forget the silly idea of selling
computers directly to ordinary people. Instead, each of these men, and
most successful people, listened to that little voice inside which will give
you the right answer.

We all have that little voice of truth, and the ability to hear it.
Too often, however, we surround ourselves with so much noise and clutter
that we cannot hear it. Or we convince ourselves that it is not what we
hear or that it is wrong because it defies logic or common knowledge. (As
we have seen, common knowledge can be somewhat fallible.) Malcolm
Gladwell's 2005 book, *Blink: The Power of Thinking Without Thinking*,
supports the notion that the rapid analysis of unconscious judgments very
often turn out better than choices that have been given more thought.
Says Gladwell:

[T]ruly successful decision making relies on a
balance between deliberate and instinctive
thinking.... Deliberate thinking is a wonderful
tool when we have the luxury of time, the help
of a computer, and a clearly defined task, and
the fruits of that type of analysis can set the stage
for rapid cognition.

[I]n good decision making, frugality matters....
[E]ven the most complicated of relationships
and problems...have an identifiable underlying
pattern.... [I]n picking up these sorts of patterns,
less is more. Overloading the decision makers
with information...makes picking up that signature
harder, not easier. To be a successful decision
maker we have to edit.

Where do we hear that voice? We do not hear it in our ears and definitely not in our brains. It can be influenced by the heart; but that, too, is not always a reliable source of right choices. Invariably, I find that **the answer is in your gut**. It is a feeling that pulls you in one direction or another. Sometimes your brain will fight it, with emotion or with logic. Where that battle occurs, it is my experience that the brain is wrong and the gut is right.

In order to hear the voice within you that knows the right answers for you, you have to **be receptive to it**. This can only occur when you are relaxed. Therefore, it is essential to build time into your day and days into your life when you can relax. **Relaxation is essential to clear thinking**. When we are rushed and frustrated, we cannot possibly be open to intuitive knowledge. We then over think and overanalyze. If you are faced with a big choice about your life's direction (go to this school or that, take this job or that, move to another state or stay where you are), there almost always is a right answer. That is, there is an answer that is right for you. And somewhere inside, you know what it is. **The You that knows the answer is prepared to tell the You that needs the answer**, but only if you are receptive to it.

How you relax is something that is different for each of us. For some people it is physical exercise—perhaps a long run in the early morning or evening. For others, it is lying with eyes closed, listening to our favorite music. For someone else it is sitting in the rocking chair just watching some pastoral scenery. How you get to that state is not as important as the fact that you get there. While it is fine to say, "I need some answers now about my life's direction, so I am going to declare a three hour time-out to relax," this is not the most effective approach. It is much better to **build routines of relaxation into your daily life**. I can definitely recommend meditation as a method to both relax and to open a window to your inner self. I was in my 20's when Transcendental Meditation was in vogue. After all, it was the late 60's and even the Beatles were off to some eastern mountain top to find "The Truth". A lot of people deride the idea of meditation as a form of voodoo, but recent scientific studies have shown that meditation actually does change brain waves and gives an induced state of deep relaxation. Taking 15 to 20 minutes every morning and late afternoon to meditate will more than make up for the "lost" time in "found" self and self awareness. [8] Most important, **when you relax you are open to hearing the inner voice.** When you hear it, **try not to fight it or too quickly overanalyze it.** When you make a choice and you decide to go with your gut, more often than not that choice will prove to be the correct one. The little voice is one way in which we are guided down the correct path. Another is described in James Redfield's bestselling book, *The Celestine Prophesy.* Thinly disguised as an adventure novel, this book is really a philosophical treatment on how to live our lives. It talks of being open to nature, and **the importance of coincidences.** It makes the point that we all encounter coincidences in life, but usually just dismiss them as coincidence and move on. Instead, Redfield suggests, we should recognize them when they occur and pay them more attention as signs of the choices we should make.[9]

A good example of seeing and seizing upon a coincidence is something that happened to my friend, Mike. Mike left communist Czechoslovakia in 1968 as a young engineer, seeking freedom in America. He learned our language, worked hard, and became a top executive of one of the largest engineering companies in the world. When Czechoslovakia rejected Communism and opened up in the early '90s, Mike listened to his inner voice which told him to leave engineering and "go east", i.e., to put his language skills and cultural knowledge to good use and make his new fortune from the many opportunities becoming available in the newly free country of his birth. He spent several years sorting out opportunities as large industries, previously government owned and run, became privatized. He was in demand as a consultant for U.S. interests wanting to figure out how to do business in what had become the Czech Republic, and for Czech companies wanting access to Western markets.

One of the opportunities Mike found, was to represent a Czech maker of trucks, in finding distributors in South America. The truck company was known for its high quality vehicles, but its business practices were well out of date. Mike dreamed of one day acquiring the company and helping set it on a path of modernization. One day, while flying on one of his frequent trips home to Florida, he sat next to another gentleman and they struck up a conversation. It seems the other man was similarly acting as a consultant for a Czech company that made generators, and he was helping them find markets in South America. He too wanted to do something more, involving ownership. They could have remarked on the coincidence and taken a nap. Instead they talked for the entire flight. Within a week, they had pooled resources. Mike is a brilliant operations guy, with good sales abilities. The other man was strongest in finance. Within a year the two of them had created a new company that ended up acquiring the truck company and beginning it on its path of improvement. Certainly there were obstacles and travails, but they were able to accomplish their goal largely because they paid attention to a coincidence, listened to the voice in their guts, and then took action on it. They could have chosen peanuts and a nap on that airplane, or having had a nice conversation, they could have chosen to wish each other well and say good bye. But they paid attention and made the choice to get together and act on their dreams. When Wayne Huizenga told me, *"{m}y whole life has been a series of wonderful coincidences or being in the right place at the right time, and that is how I got started,"* he really meant that when opportunities coincidentally appeared, he not so coincidentally acted upon them.

Some of the choices we make are fairly routine, as I have said. "Should I go to the library today or go to the mall", is not life altering. In the long run it probably will not much matter whether you go to the library or the mall....unless, of course, you consistently take the lazy path of least resistance. Even big life choices such as career options, are susceptible to rational reconciliation. In other words, it probably will not inalterably affect the course of the world if you choose to be a lawyer instead of an actor. And as I will describe in a later chapter, once you choose a path, it is generally not irreversible.

There are some choices where I believe in absolutes. I firmly believe that **there is an objective Right and Wrong**, and an objective Good or Evil. Each of us has enough moral background, be it religious training or just life experience, to know that some things are just wrong, that some actions and even some people are just evil.

When faced with such choices, we must always pick the path of Right, **always make the choice of Good over Evil.** This is too often a gray world and we become very accustomed to seeing things in shades of gray. Yet, deep in our heart (and gut) we know that there are decisions we make and actions we take that can and should be judged in black and white. You may get something you want by doing something you know to be wrong. You may win the day by siding with someone or doing something you know to be evil. Such victories are short lived and will not result in enduring success. My grandmother used to repeat an old saying that warns us: "Every dog has its day." No one who deals with the Devil comes out ahead. An alliance with evil will create a process of rot from the inside out, and the victories or accumulation of material wealth will be hollow. While I know I can provide examples of people who recklessly and ruthlessly hurt or stole from others, and achieved wealth in the process, I can point to none who enjoyed the respect of their community (as opposed to the fear or fawning), the joy of a loving family, even the self satisfaction of a job well done. Money without inner peace won't get you where you want to be. You may wonder, if the choices are so clear cut, why bad things happen to good people, and why nothing ever seems to happen to bad or mean people. Try reading Rabbi Harold Kushner's *When Bad Things Happen to Good People.* But even if you don't read it, I hope you will trust me on this: Those who choose the path of wrong or evil, must always fear the day they will be found out and have to pay for their choices. That day always comes.

When it comes to right and wrong, I might add a word of caution. There is sometimes a bright, clear line. "I should not lie, cheat, or steal." This is something we all know. If we do get ahead, through deceit or theft, such "success" is sure to be temporary. As I have said, you will be found out and success attained by such means will sooner or later reverse itself, and the downward acceleration will be at a far faster speed than the rise. There are other more blurry lines that are affected by personal religious or moral beliefs. Is embrionic stem cell research an essential scientific advance to bring about cures for millions of suffering people; or is it an unethical act that violates the sanctity of life in its earliest stages? I fall in the former camp, but I am not an ethicist. We should always be careful not to think that we have a direct line to God and ours is the only possible answer. Also, it is wise and will serve you well to remember, that no matter how much you may disagree with someone else, they are probably as sincere in their belief as you are in yours. Hence, **we should not be overly judgmental.**

Another easy choice is the choice we make (and please do not think it is anything other than a choice) to be an optimist or a pessimist. Winston Churchill once said, "I am an optimist. It does not seem too much use being anything else." We often view people and events through the prism of optimism or pessimism. If we choose the former, it is far less a burden. Churchill also said, "An optimist sees an opportunity in every calamity; a pessimist sees a calamity in every opportunity." This is so true. Looking down the same hallway, an optimist will see open doors and a pessimist will find ways to close doors or see them as closed. Which way you view it essentially comes down to a choice. Pessimism generates negative energy. **Optimism generates positive energy.** Negative energy saps creativity and forward motion. Positive energy propels us to dream new dreams and reach new heights. Is our predisposition to optimism or pessimism a function of nature or nurture? I don't know and I don't think it matters.

Whatever your predisposition, how you react to life is a choice and if you repeatedly come down on one side or the other, it is because you have developed the habit of doing so. If the habit is negative, change it to positive. One way is simply to catch yourself when any negative or pessimistic thought occurs, and repeat the opposite optimistic alternative aloud, over and over again. Then relax and move on to something else.

Madeleine Albright, former U.S. Secretary of State:

> *I do think that **there is in the United States a very much more individualistic "can do" attitude, and that people are not as dependent on the class they come from.** The mobility of American society and this kind of sense that if you really work, you can get somewhere is a very American attitude. Although I think there are more and more young people in other parts of the world that are getting the picture, for the most part, I think the older generation and some of these countries have a hard time adapting to them.*

She also believes that that "can do" attitude very often translates to the reality:

> *I think so. I really think that in my case what happened was that my parents were very directed or focused, I guess is the right word, in terms*

of making it in America. They never thought that Czechoslovakia would be free and that they would, at least in their life times, that they would be able to go back, and so they were bound and determined and they instilled that in us, at times in a way that I found difficult. I mean, when we moved to Denver I had gone to public school. My father then heard that scholarships were offered in this small private school I had no desire to go, but he made me go, and it made a big difference because I think I got a very good education, and it lead to a scholarship for college. It was one of those things that, this is what you do and this is how you have to work hard, and so there was very much of work ethic.

Jeb Bush, Governor of Florida:

You've got to be [an optimist] in this. I mean, again **as Governor, if you are pessimistic it cascades out, it impacts everything and everybody. I think it's really important to be optimistic and to have...I have a deep and abiding faith with the dynamic nature of life and individuals. People that are equipped, you know, armed with knowledge, armed with certain character traits can achieve far more they can ever imagine and that's based on an underlying bed of optimism.** *I had, in government, it's funny, not funny, it's a fact that young people without having lot of experience are put into positions of incredible responsibilities. It's one of the few places in life where that's the case and one of my acquired skills over time is recognizing talent and then encouraging people to fulfill their talent, which they may not have known that they had inside of them. One of the greatest joys I've had is to see people that work under high pressure situations; you know it's 2:00 on Friday, and we have a joke in our office that around 4:00 some horrible thing on Friday afternoons always happens. Every week we have to wait and see what it's going to be this week, but horrific tragedies do happen...4 hurricanes in an 8 week period, whatever it is, these young people, mostly young, have really performed way beyond what they thought they could. If I had a pessimistic attitude and a cynical attitude, I don't think the best of the people around me would have emerged.*

Absolutely **being principled certainly is part of it; being optimistic is critical.** *You know in a public setting particularly* *because people watch, you know, they may be watching with their peripheral vision, but they watch.... I remember, for me to use an example, would be one of the things that President Carter did that probably doomed his Presidency was the "malaise" speech. And it's a classic example. People don't want to be told their life's going to be worse. I mean, it can't be phony and fake. It has to be grounded in some basis of truth, but they want to be inspired, to be better, and do better and whether you're a dad to a kid, or the head of a law firm to the junior partners, or a Governor to a state, it's important to be able to communicate a hopeful optimistic message.*

Nina Tassler, President of CBS Entertainment:

*I think that [optimism is] something that I was born with. I don't think that it was something that I could attribute to any particular event in my life. Ironically when my mother tells stories of how I behaved as a child or how I reacted to things as a child, it's that **I had a very optimistic outlook on life. I equate optimism with passion and when I approach something or set out to do something, I have a sense that things will turn out for the best and my attitude toward something is that things will be positive and I think there will be a positive outcome.** So, I have a very high level of energy and the prospect of something being successful or something being creatively fulfilling is exciting to me, and that manifests itself in enthusiasm and passion. That's not to say that I don't feel disappointed if something doesn't come to fruition, or something doesn't really achieve the goals that I've set out, but I think part of wanting something a great deal or feeling very strongly or passionately is the fact that there will be disappointments. But, I think that I can feel disappointment with the same degree of intensity that I can feel passion, but again, all of that is a result of commitment and giving yourself to something 100%.*

One manifestation of whether we are an optimist or pessimist is how we view other people. Do you distrust other people until they prove themselves trustworthy? Or do you trust them until they prove themselves untrustworthy? As a child I learned from my father that people who are always distrustful are never really happy and place roadblocks to their own success. So, I prefer to **trust until proven wrong**. Making this choice means that inevitably, there will be times when you are disappointed. So what? You will be a lot happier if you take that risk with people and seek out the best in them rather than expecting the worst and taking satisfaction in confirming it.

Every day we face choices of how we view people, events, and words. It is these very choices that help shape whether we will be happy and successful. As Deepak Chopra points out, if someone says something insulting or offensive, it is our choice whether we will be insulted or offended, or not. Think, how much better off we are if the choice is to not be insulted or offended.

Parents often find it is easy to upset a teenage son or daughter. Perhaps that is because the pre-college teenager tends to be intensely self-centered. They see most statements as being about them. They could be so much happier and calmer if they would stop and realize that a comment about clothing is about clothing—not about them. A comment about food is just about food—not about them. In other words, there are choices made on how we view other people's actions and words. Too often we get into the habit of personalizing them and making it "about me." This is a barrier to success. It is not easy, but if we could learn to **choose not to take offense** when hearing something offensive, we would definitely find smoother sailing on the sea of life. One of my father's long standing pieces of advice is: "smile and the world smiles with you." He suggests that if someone says something nasty, you can just smile and say, "thank you." This serves two functions: you have chosen not to have a harmful negative emotion, and the other person will be upset at having failed to upset you.

So make those daily choices, and choose wisely. Keep it simple with some of those choices: **right over wrong, good over evil, optimism over pessimism.** With the others, you are apt to be pulled in conflicting directions, so while it might never be completely simple you can simplify it if you learn to relax and go with your gut.

REFLECTIONS AND APPLICATIONS—CHAPTER 6

1. Do you have trouble making important decisions? Why do you think that is? What steps can you take now to correct that?
2. On what factors do you base your choices? Can you see a consistent pattern?
3. What means of relaxation are best for you? Do you schedule time each day for them? Start finding time in your schedule.
4. How important is morality in your life? Would you have fewer regrets if you considered morality as a guiding factor in your life?

CHAPTER 7
THE FOURTH SECRET: NEVER QUIT

There is a story I told my children as they were growing up. It is about Winston Churchill who rose to power in England, after many setbacks and defeats to his ambition for leadership. Every time he made some advance professionally or politically, it seemed that he was beaten back. Until one day, seemingly out of nowhere, he was chosen to be Prime Minister at the time of England's greatest danger; a time when its very survival (and that of the Western world) was at stake. Fortunately for England and for all of us who find the German language difficult to learn, Churchill persevered until he got the prize he had sought, and then proved to be the right man for the time, giving his country the strength to persevere through its most difficult hours.

As the story goes, after Churchill's leadership helped defeat the Nazis against overwhelming odds and free Europe, he was asked to speak at the graduation exercise of a U.S. College. The President of the college gave a glowing introduction, and then Churchill, aging and overweight, lumbered up to the podium. He looked around at the student audience and finally uttered two words: "Never quit." Then he sat down. The college President was a little surprised, and, recovering, he said, "Mr. Churchill, would you care to expand on your remarks?" Again, the Great Man slowly rose and approached the podium. This time he said, "Never, never, never quit." End of speech.

That is the moral even if the story is somewhat invented or embellished. In fact, he was speaking to his countrymen when he actually said this:

> Never give in, never give in, never
> never, never, never—in nothing, great
> or small, large or petty—never give in
> except to convictions of honour and
> good sense.

If there is a single characteristic of successful people, it is their steadfastness, the determination to keep going. [And, according to my daughter, Marni, they give good quotes in a single sentence.] They do not quit in the face of difficulty. They **do not quit when the going gets tough.** They do not quit when others discourage them. Napolean Hill, an advisor to President Roosevelt during the Depression, wrote several books including an extensive book called *Laws of Success.* He had spent many years studying a large number of people who had become financially successful. Comparing two of those, Thomas Edison (who had conducted several thousand unsuccessful experiments before finally getting it right with the invention of the light bulb) and Henry Ford, Hill said: "I found no quality save persistence, in either of them, that even remotely suggested the major source of their stupendous achievements."

The same lesson is heard from a modern Stateswoman, **Madeleine Albright.** I asked if she had learned the importance of perseverance from her parents' experiences. She said:

> *There's no question. I've written in my memoir that **the thing about my parents that was so interesting, was that they made the abnormal seem normal.** We had gone through so many ups and downs, and so many moves, and they made it seem as if that was kind of a normal life, and they themselves worked very very hard. My father, who had been an Ambassador and I remember so well, living in an Embassy and all kinds of butlers and chauffeurs and everything, and then **we came to the United States and we basically had nothing.** He had to start a career over and persevered in teaching and writing in a foreign language. My mother, who had been a daughter out of a fairly well to do family, as I said, had already learned to take care of everything and work hard when we were in England during the War, but then we came to the United States, she went to work as a secretary. **They both persevered very hard and they basically, in looking back on it, were pretty upbeat about everything and very grateful to be here.** So their approach to everything, I think, really made the difference. I mean, we were just so glad to be here, that was the main thing....*
>
> *You know, this has come up in a variety of ways, but when I was like 5 or 6, we were in England and I got a report card in which it*

*said "Madeleine is discouraged by first difficulties". My father took me aside because he was very loving but strict, he said "I never want to hear that about you again" and I do think that that is the advice that I would give people. It's that every part of our lives, getting a job in the first place, and it's pretty hard to go in and sit there in interviews and try to figure out what the person interviewing you wants, and how do you present the fact that you went to college as a resume? People ask you what your experience is before you have any experience. So I do think it's a model that's true anyway. I mean, **you cannot be discouraged by first difficulties** and it's hard. But that is something I have found very useful for myself and certainly for my own daughters and friends. I spent a lot of time with young people, and I think that one of the things that is really important is that people have overblown ideas of what they are capable of when they're 22 years old. Part of what has happened is that, in college these days, there are so many incredible opportunities for internships and travel abroad and all kinds of opportunities in the summers and then the entry level jobs are not that interesting...*

*I mean, you just graduated from college with a great degree that you can't get a job right away in your field, and so you go do something that isn't so great; or you even get a job in your chosen field but you're not making policy, you're making coffee. I think that people have to understand that you have to pay your dues. **I've paid my dues. I worked very hard in a whole host of other things that took me a long time. I got paid back pretty well, but I really do think that it's just this kind of sense that nobody owes you a living, nobody owes you a job.** The fact that you were fortunate enough to go to college is great, and some cases you have to pay back loans and in some cases your parents did it. But on the whole, you have to start out there and a good transcript is not enough to pay your dues.*

Public life must either be a great teacher or else it attracts people who have learned great lessons, because the same message was a part of my interview with **Jeb Bush**. I asked him about narrowly losing his first race for Governor in 1994 and how he felt about it, and how he had bounced right back to run again in 1998:

*That's a great question. In fact I think **the greatest lessons I've learned in my life have not been the successes but the defeats.** The '94 experience was an awesome one for me because we, I started really with a lot of people having preconceived notions about me. They weren't necessarily...I had to work hard to earn people's respect because of the fact that I was the son of a President running for Governor not having worked my way up as you said. So I learned a lot on that experience and loss was very hurtful. I didn't immediately make up my mind that I was going to run. It took 2 solid years, but I took the time to stop...It didn't take long for me to realize that blaming others or blaming dirty campaigns...whatever, all the things that people around me were saying, it didn't take me long to realize that that really was irrelevant. That I should use this as an opportunity to be better as a person...{T}ake the opportunity to grow as a person, which I did. I went back to work and back to business, but I also had my faith which strengthened me. I vowed to be a stronger, better husband, better Dad. I gained humility, it's a great way to get humility losing an election.*

Persistence. Refusal to concede failure. The determination to keep going. Can this be such a critical component of success? Obviously, it can. Remember the quote in an earlier chapter from billionaire, Ross Perot: "I've found that **successful people just don't know when they have failed.**"

I would not want to give the impression that there isn't another side to this. There is an old (sort of) joke, that the definition of insanity is doing the same thing over and over again, and expecting a different result. However, by persistence we are not really talking about doing the same thing over and over. We are talking about **holding on to the same goal, pursuing it vigorously, maintaining focus and self-confidence,** while rejecting detours and detractors. It does not mean we do not experiment or try a different route—in fact, experimentation may well be an essential component. "If at first you don't succeed, try and try again" is an old saying founded in folklore that precedes most known success literature. If it took Edison 9,950 experimental tries to get his light bulb to work, consider where the world would be today had he given up at 9,949. I might be writing this with a ballpoint pen by candlelight.

Remember the story of Mrs. Evans that I described in the first chapter? She was the old lady who told me to bet on the favorite horse to "show" in every race. I recall asking her if she ever deviated from this. Generally not, she said. Too many people go for the thrill of betting on the horse that will win, but if you deviate from the plan you will introduce too much of an element of chance. Randomness and emotion will thwart your success. However, sometimes, because you are at the track every day and you get to know people, you will occasionally hear that the regular jockey is sick, or the horse is lame, and that is when you can apply logic and deviate from the plan. So, whether at the race track (which, again, I am not counseling be your path to riches) or football, or in business—**have a game plan and stick to it.**

It is possible to find historical evidence to support the notion that success goes to those who persevere, in every avenue of life. How many politicians have lost election after election before finally winning? Abraham Lincoln lost nearly every election he entered, for local office, for Congress, for the U.S. Senate, before he won the presidency. Although the occasional great invention is serendipitous (Eureka, I have found it!), the product of keen observation or dumb luck, so many more are like Edison's, the result of dogged pursuit of an idea through an awful lot of experimentation.

Many entrepreneurs struck out before finding their riches. Ted Arison, the founder of Carnival Cruise lines, twice went bankrupt before starting Carnival and becoming both a billionaire and philanthropist. He did not slink out of bankruptcy and say, "I guess I am not cut out for business, so I might as well take that job as a clerk." He had his vision and he persevered. One of the most difficult parts of getting a book published is for a new author to find a literary agent. Most publishers do not want to consider manuscripts submitted without an agent, and most agents want to represent only published authors (because, as Willie Sutton said when asked why he robs bank, "that is where the money is."). Discouraged when her first book had been rejected by two agents she had sent it to, one aspiring young author I know, spoke with best selling novelist Brad Meltzer. Brad told her that he had received 24 rejection letters on his first book, and they are all now framed in a plaque on his wall. His advice: if you believe in yourself and in your writing, and you are rejected 24 times, send it to a 25th...and do not wait to start writing your second book. Begin NOW working on that next book because writers write. Similarly, Nora Roberts is a famous romance novelist who, according to Forbes Magazine, earns $60million a year from her writing. Yet her first six books were flat out rejected. She was not deterred. She kept on writing.

Brad Meltzer, novelist:

> *When I was writing in law school...I wrote my first book before I got to law school. It got me 24 rejection letters, and at that point there were only 20 publishers, and I had 24 people tell me to give it up. Telling me some people were sending me the same letter twice to make sure I got the point.*

But, I said, you wouldn't take the point?

> *I wouldn't take the point, of course. I'm lawyer and what happened was, I said if they don't like that book then I'm going to write another, and if they don't like that book, I'm going to write another and if they don't like that book, I'm going to write another, and the same week I got my 23rd and 24th rejection letter, it was exactly the same week that I started my next book which became The Tenth Justice. I started that book at Columbia. Columbia was kind enough, they gave me credit for writing that book, which was they said, if you can find a professor who will give you independent study credit, we will give you credit for the book, and I found...Professor Kellis Barker, who passed away a couple years back. When I saw that his class was called "Jazz and the Law", I said I found my guide, and not only did they give me credit for it, but when I was photocopying the manuscript to send it out and I didn't have any money to go and photocopy a 500 page manuscript to 20 different places, they actually...I bought all this toner cartridge and I asked "can I use your copiers, I'll supply the paper and the toner," and the law school, at that point the Dean of Students, said give me the transcript, we'll do it for you.... That was the encouragement you need when you start writing.... I've been very fortunate that I've always been told, even if I couldn't do it, that I should at least try, and I think that was so much of what influenced me over time....*

*I think one other writer said to me once and it really helped me when I was writing my second book, that he said "it's ok to admit that it's hard." I think with writing particular people have this fantasy that you're sitting there and you're drinking pina coladas on the beach and then you type out a page and then you go back to the beach and it's such a—you feel, I feel so lucky that I get to do this and I realize to me this is not work. Work is something that puts calluses on your hands and dirt under your fingernails and this is not that. And so to me the fact that I get to do this, I just, you know I feel like any complaint about it is just pathetic. But one writer said to me, "it's ok to admit it's hard sometimes." You know, if it were easy everyone would do it, and that was helpful to me. I think the best advice though, was what I'd look back on the experience. I mean, as I was saying before, **I got 24 rejection letters and 24 people told me to give it up, and I look back on the experience, I just think it means you have to keep following it and chasing that dream. It almost, it sounds cliched, but the only way to find that dream is to chase it and so I always say to anyone, don't let anyone tell you no.** That's the best advice. **Don't let anyone tell you no. Life is just subjective.** What if a few people can tell me to give it up; doesn't mean any one of them are right, and as long as you live by that, hopefully, you will eventually find what you are chasing.*

Every person will face setbacks. **Every great quest will encounter obstacles.** Sometimes the obstacles will seem insurmountable. But the great achievers keep pushing, rejecting these setbacks as defining events. Madame Curie, reflecting on her very difficult life as a child and young adult, wrote: "Never let one be beaten down by persons or by events." That is advice worth remembering when things are not going as we would like. One of the great common themes of the successful is to believe in yourself.

Bob Graham, former Governor of and U.S. Senator from Florida:

You don't want to be isolated because lots of times the criticism is both well intended and appropriate. But on the other hand, you are responsible ultimately to yourself and you don't want to be freaked out and become just a wind thing spinning by the last person who made a comment, either positive or negative.

Nina Tassler, President of CBS Entertainment:

> *You know what, at that point* [early in her career} *I was trying to be an actor an actor trained as an actor, you really had to have a fair amount of self confidence in order to go out and suffer the difficult process of going through auditioning and rejection. You build up over a period of time, a fair amount of self-confidence, but this was just something I felt very comfortable doing.*

I remember having some very hard times during the recession of 1990-92. The law business was doing all right, but other investments we had were in deep trouble. I was in debt and faced with the prospect of banks calling in their loans. (This experience undoubtedly made me much more debt averse in the future, and while there are sound business reasons to incur debt, I am a big believer in avoiding debt in your personal life.) Many well-meaning friends counseled me to give up some of the business investments, such as my wife's business that was very dependent on the economy and was losing money and had eaten up our savings. Our decision, though, was to continue to find creative ways to keep going. It was not easy. At least four or five times a day, often looking into the mirror to convince the guy looking back, I said to myself out loud, "I will survive!" Survive we did. A couple of years later that business was hugely successful, making a lot of money, providing great satisfaction; and we were completely out of debt.[10] As Joe Torre, Manager of the New York Yankees has said: **"Tough times don't last, tough people do."**

I can think of another classic example, from my own experience, of the importance of persevering. I was elected to the Florida Legislature in 1972. At that time a State Representative was allowed to have one secretary **or** one aide. My first year I had an aide. I soon realized that I did not really need someone to help me with drafting or following the progress of legislation, or deciding how to communicate with the people in my district. What I needed was someone to help us get the work out. So, I decided that in my second year, I would hire a secretary instead of the aide. Around that time, a young man who had been active in Young Democrats and in local political campaigns, graduated college. His name was Ronnie.

Ronnie came to me and said he wanted to be my aide. I told him that I was not going to hire an aide, that I needed a secretary. A week later he came back and again asked to be my aide. I said, "Ronnie, I am sure you would be a great aide, but I don't need an aide; I need a secretary." Over the next couple of weeks this dialogue was repeated several times, as he kept returning and pushing for the opportunity to work for me. Finally, he came to me and said: "Look, I want to be your aide, and I know you want a secretary. Hire me as your aide and I will hire a secretary from my salary." What could I say to that? So, I hired him, and he hired a secretary from his fairly modest government salary. After a while I came to see what a good aide he was, took pity, and took over the salary of the secretary. Ronnie got what he wanted because he would not take "no" for an answer. Later, he went to law school (that, too, could make a pretty good tale of perseverance), and today he is one of the top lobbyists in Florida, getting new clients and results for his clients through that same unstoppable combination of high energy and perseverance.

In another lesson I learned from someone I hired, I once hired a bright young lawyer who had interviewed well. Later he told me that he had five rejection letters from me, where I had declined to interview him. It is another example of perseverance, but also of the importance of timing. However good his resume, if there was no opening, I was not going to hire him. When the opening was there, so was he, because he had not been deterred by rejection.

I remember reading a similar story about comedian, Eddie Murphy. A producer of *Saturday Night Live* got a cold call from Murphy asking for an audition. The producer said he did not have any openings and was not conducting auditions at that time. Murphy, who was out of work and calling from a pay phone, called him every day for a week, arguing that he would be great on the show and should have an audition. The producer, finally finding it easier to give an audition than to continue getting the daily phone calls, agreed to let him come in. The rest is, of course, show business history.

Another show business example is actress, Salma Hayek. Speaking with graduate acting students on an episode of *Inside the Actors' Studio*, a student asked if she had ever lost a role because of her accent. "Are you kidding," she responded. "A thousand times. But look where I am." In other words, she had, against all the odds and all the nay-sayers, persevered and came out on top. "**Embrace adversity**," she told the students, "because **it is your best teacher**." Show business, being the difficult, competitive field it is, has more than its share of good examples of the need for belief in yourself and perseverance in the face of adversity. Actor Tom Hanks's high school drama coach, in an interview, said he had never cast Hanks in good parts because he didn't think he was any good. Asked about Hanks's subsequent success, the teacher said (in a rare display of humility), "I guess I was wrong." Actress Sigourney Weaver was told by her Yale drama professor that she had no talent and would not make it. Fortunately for both their amazing and durable careers, and the delight of the movie-going public, neither star was deterred by people who tried to douse their dreams.

The idea of embracing adversity was also a theme of my discussion **with Jorge de Cespedes**, President of PharMed:

> *Yeah,* **you use it** [adversity] **to your advantage.** *I remember nearly 20 years ago winning our first bid, major bid at Jackson Memorial Hospital. It was us and four companies, publicly traded companies, that made presentations. It was a piece of business for about $6,000,000 at that time. We were just starting out. Our annual revenues were maybe $1,500,000 and here we're going after a $6,000,000 piece of business. We made our presentation, and I guess it was passionate and good enough that the business was given to us. Carlos and I looked at each other, when we were awarded the bid and said "now what? What the hell do we do now? How do we support the $6,000,000 piece of business?" Credit wise or with vendors. The vendor in question was Johnson & Johnson and our normal orders with them were about $10,000 a month, so they were quite surprised when we placed our first order of $250,000. Well, we can't ship you and this...and so the whole thing is like, I believe that if you haven't had the right life training...forget your college training. I mean, I know what the book says, but you know you have to have the life training. A lot of people a) wouldn't have gone after the bid; b) after they got the bid, they would have rolled over and played dead the first time J&J said we can't ship you that kind of merchandise, you are not credit worthy for that kind of merchandise.*

"No" isn't acceptable, I suggested. He went on:

> **No** *is* **not acceptable.** *Listen, we won the bid; we are a distributor; how are we going to work this out? What do you need? The next*

THERE'S ALWAYS ROOM AT THE TOP

thing you know people are flying down here; are you are willing to put your house as collateral? Yes I am. Your wife's signature. Yes she signs. **You just, you believe in yourself enough that that type of stuff doesn't faze you.** *Things haven't changed any in that sense. The numbers have just gotten a lot bigger and getting people to believe in you, to give you a $250,000 credit versus now, you are going into $25,000,000 deals.* **It still takes the same amount of effort and energy. Just the numbers are different....**

You also know you have to accept failure once in a while. Not be afraid of it. It's again related to sports. You know in sports there is typically another game tomorrow. *OK, so you went 0-4 today. Well you get to go to bat again tomorrow morning early and our season never ends. In the real sports world, there's the Superbowl and that ends the season, or there is the World Series, or there is the NBA Championships. In the business world you have a game every single day of your life. Even on Saturdays and Sundays. You know, my wife often tells me, "you never stop selling". It's a lifestyle.*

Writer, actor, comedian Woody Allen has said that 80% of success in life is just showing up. That is a metaphor for perseverance. Keep on going, keep on showing up. Others will drop out of the race and you will finish if you simply never give up. In one of his classic success writings late in the 19th Century, Orison Swett Marden wrote, "Show me a really great triumph that is not the reward of persistence."

Sure, it is possible to try something once, get a break or two and be an instant success. This, however, is by far the exception. Those who dream of and wait for such a break are, almost invariably, failures condemned to the bottom of life's barrel. Those who set their sights on a goal and take persistent action end up the winners. In *The Power or Focus*, the authors say: "If you take a close look at people who are truly successful in life, you will find one characteristic trait in abundance.... We call it Consistent Persistence." I cannot agree more, and in fact, if you speak with anyone who has achieved enduring success in virtually any field of endeavor you are likely to find total agreement on this point.

Why then are so many people unable to keep going? It is back to the choices they make. Back to "isn't it easier said than done?" And, yes, it is easier said than done. The reason is that life often conspires to put up roadblocks in our path. There is rarely a shortage of obstacles to any new and worthwhile pursuit. **Sometimes it seems we are being tested with adversity at every turn.** There are always people around, often people with your best interest at heart, or who purport to have your best interest at heart, who will tell you that your dream is unrealistic; or that what you want cannot be done, or you are making things unnecessarily difficult for yourself and you should give up and try something else. These temptations to retreat can be very appealing when you are tired or hungry and see no end in sight. So what should you do? **Believe in yourself and your dreams and keep going, with determination and every bit of energy you can muster.**

REFLECTIONS AND APPLICATIONS—CHAPTER 7

1. Have you ever encountered adversity? How did you deal with it? Have you ever benefited from it?
2. Do you find rejection causes you to stop trying? Find one small rejection you have encountered and push past it as if it never happened.

CHAPTER 8
THE FIFTH SECRET:KEEP YOUR EYE ON THE DOUGHNUT

It is impossible to overstate the importance of Focus. By focus I mean the **determined effort to stay on task**, the discipline to keep your energies directed at the goal and not to be deterred by the competing demands for your attention. When I was much younger, I heard a silly little poem that expressed this valuable life lesson. It goes:

As you travel down the path of life,

whatever be your goal,

keep your eye upon the doughnut

and not upon the hole.

It is so easy to let your focus slip, to gaze into the hole of the doughnut and find an endless, empty space that detracts from the true mission. Yet, every successful person will tell you that **right alongside perseverance as an essential characteristic, is focus.** While you do not want to slip over the line to obsession, I do believe it is important to come as close as possible to that line without sacrificing a normal and healthy life.

Undoubtedly, you have heard of this one in some form or another. When working on a school paper, have you let yourself be interrupted with a social telephone call, or going to the mall with a friend, or (if you are under 25) Instant Messaging alongside the paper on your computer? Of course you have. And your parents may have chided you about the **discipline** necessary to complete the task before moving on. Whether you kept your focus and finished the project; or took a break assuming you can get right back to it (or worse, instant messaged three different conversations simultaneously while working on it, assuming that these distractions would not adversely affect the final product), came down to a choice you made. Every baseball player has heard since early childhood that to hit the ball you must not take your eye off the ball. That means **total concentration on the task at hand.**

ALAN S. BECKER

In planning for success, this can be even more difficult. The reason is that we are not talking about a single swing of the bat, where you get several tries until there are three strikes. We are not talking about one paper to be turned in that constitutes a small part of a grade in a course that won't matter a whole lot ten years from now. We are talking about your life and the direction you want it to take. That often means **deferred gratification**, i.e., sacrifice now for the reward that comes later. You want to excel in a field? You want to be well-known for your accomplishments? You want to attain wealth or security? Then you must start with the choice to **impose the discipline on yourself**: that is focus. Your waking (and sometimes your sleeping) thoughts must be directed toward the objective, and your actions must follow. In writing this book, I took a two week hiatus to concentrate on other things—the immediate career obligations of a law practice and family obligations. I guess, though, my mind was still focused where it had to be. Fast asleep one night, I dreamt the title of a new chapter I had not previously outlined as well as the entire first two pages of text. I awoke in the morning remembering it, and added it to my outline. If your goal is going to be reached, it should reasonably consume your waking and sleeping thoughts, and you must take action on those thoughts.[11]

Madeleine Albright, former Secretary of State:

> *I think that often people who get something too easily in the beginning don't know quite why. Some of it isn't just raw talent, some of it has to, you never know...but then they get disappointed when it doesn't last. It's a lot easier to work your way up, than to be up and then go down, and so I think the time is worth it....**If you start at the top, it's a little harder to get real satisfaction out of how you got there. And part of success, to go back to your original question, part of success is having gotten there. Of having realized that as a result of hard work, and determination, and focus, and just slugging it out, is you got there rather than having somebody hand you some great thing at the beginning.***

Bob Graham, former Governor of and U.S. Senator from Florida:

> *Well, I can say what I try to do is to think in goals which aren't extremely tangible but which cover the space that you're interested in. For instance, when I was elected as Senate, I said, there are several*

126

areas that I want to spend most of my time. One, Florida is more affected than the average state; second—it's an area in which I have a personal interest and believe I can make a difference. [Those were: Latin America, the elderly, growth issues, the issue of the borders, and the environment.] *So, those were the five issues that I most focused on.*

I asked **Susan Story**, CEO of Gulf Power Co., if you are going to be successful do you have to know how to stay on task and maintain focus, and she replied:

*Absolutely, because you know, **no results, plus excuses do not equal results.** Really, in most of things we do, the bottom line results and the behaviors on which we got there, that's the most important thing. People may have different ways to do them, as long as they are honest and ethical and they get the job done, who cares how they do it? And as an engineer, believe it or not, I don't believe in micromanaging, and I actually like the strategy part better than the day to day nuts and bolts. But with an engineering background, I can do the nuts and bolts if I need to.* [Susan described a negotiation she led involving construction of a power plant where hundreds of millions of dollars were in dispute.] ***Focus, objective, but I also had the homework.** I had teams of people who got me the data and I could show, they had built part of a power plant and were saying that had more than they had done, and they weren't meeting budgets and schedules. We had done it before and I could sit there and I could refute every single thing they said factually to the point that they knew, if it went to arbitration, number one, they wouldn't get their money, number two probably won't win. So I think there's a lot to be said about that in terms of team work, in terms of knowing your stuff. It's not enough to be a ra, ra, cheerleader, which I do think I'm good at. You also have to have the substance and the confidence to know what you're doing, and to know how to drive to a result that makes the difference.*

Putting the same principle in a spiritual context in *The Seven Spiritual Laws of Success*, Chopra describes this as "holding your attention to the intended outcome with such unbending purpose that you absolutely refuse to allow obstacles to consume and dissipate the focused quality of your attention."

In other words, no hocus pocus, just focus, focus, focus.

Different people have different approaches to maintain focus. I asked **Governor Jeb Bush** how he maintains focus, observing that he send his emails awfully early in the morning. He replied,

Well, first of all I don't {maintain focus} when I'm in Tallahassee. I go home early. It's important for me to get out of the office because the office is the place where we get bombarded with, as I said, other people's agenda. I like being with my wife. I work at home. When I go home, I walk home normally, at least in non-summer months, and I'll be home at 6:00. I wake up early, but I'm with my wife and that grounds me. I strive to not fret about every detail, which was hard to do in the beginning…. It's not that I ignore those things {that come up daily}. It's that I have confidence in the people that are working on it, so I don't get obsessed or consumed by the tyranny of the moment. If you look for the tyranny of the present, you know, what's in front of you, you can't focus on the longer term things and leaders need to lead, they don't need to micromanage.

Again, it is of course much easier for me to counsel such discipline than for you to impose it on yourself on a sustained basis, day after day, week after week, month after month. You do it by making it a habit. You do it by reminding yourself, every time your actions or your thoughts get off track, to bring them back to where they have to be. A key to being able to do this is to understand and have the ability to **compartmentalize**. By this, I am referring to developing the ability to separate the things that happen in your life, and not allow those that occur in different categories to cross over and distract from your concentration on the things that matter most to your quest for success.

We all have different parts of our lives and thoughts running simultaneously. We have the grand goal, the day-to-day business, the love-life or family life, the immediate activity such as shopping for food or driving somewhere. If we did not pay attention to shopping for food, we would starve. If we did not pay attention to driving, we would likely end up in an accident. The point is, though, that all of these can exist simultaneously so long as we designate a place in our consciousness for each. If we are with our family, even if the time is short, then give the family the full benefit of that time without worrying about the grand goal or the shopping list. Do not let a setback in business color your family time, or conversely, let a set back in your love-life so overwhelm your thoughts or actions that it takes from your pursuit of success. Each has its place, its compartment if you will, and the ability to keep each in its place is what will let you **remain focused on the goal even as life happens all about you.**

Jeb Bush, Governor of Florida:

> *I use the tools of productivity that exist now that Governors didn't have before. I have the greatest technology and that allows me to focus on the details as well as stay focused on the bigger things. I work really hard and I have good people that work for me that are my extended reach. So, I'm not saying that I've got it down pat, and I'm not saying it's a science. It's more of an art and sometimes I get too distracted from the bigger things, but I'll tell you one thing I do. I have once a week a day that we call "Time to be Governor Day" because it got to the point where…I would be weeks on end without having any free time to think or to make calls or to check in on people or to worry about my agenda. I was worried about everybody else's. So a couple years ago we started this thing called "Time to be Governor Day". It's normally Wednesday and I start it by mentoring, which I've done for the last six years. I'm mentor of a little school kid. That kind of gets my head clear and once I struggle with the Geometry and Math for 7th graders or 8th graders, then I go into the office and I have a meeting with my Chief of Staff and four Deputy Chiefs of Staff. That typically takes an hour and we go through the agenda and the rest of the day is what I want it to be. So at least one day a week, I'm Governor and that has helped a lot—that has helped a tremendous amount.*

Jorge de Cespedes, President, PharMed:

> *There's definitely a few things to execution. I think you have to ask for the business…. Next, returning calls. Returning calls. Something as simple as that. It's OK to call somebody back to say, I'm not ready for you, I'm not ready to give you an answer or no I don't want to do this right now. But you've got to call them back. You've got to respond to that and most businesses go down not because there is a problem. Lack of responsiveness will kill them. If one follows through on a regular*

basis, the customer, whether it be your clients or customer, they know they can count on you; they know you are going to give them a response to an inquiry.

Bob Graham, former Governor of and U.S. Senator from Florida:

*My father carried a notebook on the dairy farm. When he saw a sick cow, he'd write it down to remind himself to do something about the cow. I had done it on a disorganized basis until I began running for Governor in 1977. I realized I was being inundated with people, many of whom I was meeting for the first time, and they wanted to ask me to do something or described some problem they had. Particularly when I was doing these work days I needed some way, while I was working, to be able to take notes about what people were saying. So I started using these in an organized way with several different components. The first book is what I call a log. I write down everyday what I do. I get kidded because of the minutiae of something like this. But, interestingly, in writing this book {Intelligence Matters}, there were several times that the very fact I had written what might have been referred to as minutiae became the color, the fabric of a story. Then **I'm a list taker. I write down the things that I want to do day by day and then use that as a checklist.** Then I write down names of people, whatever information they may have. If I'm attending a meeting that I think is important I will not take stenographic notes, but I will write enough to be able to recall the major points we cover; and particularly I can keep a list of what I call my follow up list which are the things I committed to do in that meeting so that I can be sure that I fulfilled my obligations afterwards. I find them to be a very effective means of organizing a life which otherwise could get very disorderly. Frankly one of the surprises of my Washington days has been the fact that particularly journalists there find me to be sort of an eccentric type. I can think of being a lot things, but eccentric was not one of them. If some people said look, you're taking a lot of heat from the press about these notebooks, do you want to quit. I said I don't care what they say. They are valuable to me and I'm not going to discontinue what other people don't understand.*

There are many things that occur every day, some annoying, some tragic, some encouraging, and many just downright distracting. Yet, for your own well being (physical and mental health), your serenity, and... most significantly, your ability to remain on track heading steadfastly toward your goals, you must be able to put those daily events in perspective. Viewed with the proper perspective you will find that most are relatively insignificant. When one of my kids or one of my employees comes to me all upset over something that has occurred or something that has been said, I usually ask them to apply this test: **will this matter a year from now?** If the answer is "No", then why spend much time and mental energy worrying about it. You can also ask, "will this matter in a week?" and usually get the same answer.

Recently, my older daughter reminded me that throughout her life I always advised her, "Don't sweat the small stuff." That was long before someone, obviously a whole lot smarter than I am, wrote a book (and then a series of books) by that title giving the same sage advice. The point is, there are too many real things in life for us to be concerned with, and we should not spend so much of our attention on distractions that serve no useful purpose but often make us unhappy or resentful or fill us with doubts.[12] My rule of thumb is that I will give a situation or occurrence mental attention if I can do something about it. If not, then I accept what is, and move along. Banishing concerns with small distractions will help with the all-important objective of maintaining focus.

REFLECTIONS AND APPLICATIONS—CHAPTER 8

1. Do you "sweat the small stuff"?
2. Can you develop and encourage focus?
3. What interruptions do you allow to intrude upon your priority activities? What is your major distraction from the task at hand?

CHAPTER 9
THE SIXTH SECRET: HERE IS ALWAYS ROOM AT THE TOP

It is an interesting phenomenon that in any field of endeavor, **the bottom ranks are crowded.** There may be a million lawyers, but only a handful who stand out in their specialty or in their firms. There may be a million actors, but only a small number who *stand for something* and who stand out in the public mind. So, if you are shooting for success in a crowded field, it is best to **set your sights where there is less of a crowd, and that is always at the top.**

Believe it or not, it takes just as much energy to enter a job or a profession and perform at acceptable levels, as it does to reach the top of the heap. The biggest difference is that the people who reach the top have learned and applied the lessons of the preceding chapters: they have learned that it is better to set your goals high, to believe in your ability to achieve them, and to conduct yourself in the ways necessary to do so. They are not afraid to take the chance of failure. They are not concerned with the assessment of other people that it is difficult, perhaps too difficult, to reach such heights. They are willing to put in the relatively small amount of extra effort that is required. They visualize themselves scaling the mountain, and standing victorious at the peak.

Those who set their sights at the top are usually the only ones who reach the top. Still, not everyone who sets out to reach the top will do so. Nonetheless, the mere setting of that goal and pursuit of it, will virtually assure that they will end up at a much higher point than the others in the game. There is only one President of the United States, but those who enter politics and set their sights on being President, are almost entirely the pool from which we get Governors and Senators. **Bob Graham** told me, less than half facetiously, "I think there is no city councilman in the smallest village who doesn't, once elected begin to think about [being President]." John Kerry missed by a mere percentage point (a virtual "landslide" for George W. Bush in this era of divided electorate and minority Presidents), but it was that long-time ambition that assured he could rise to be a member of the United States Senate and a major figure in that body. Had he entered politics with the view that, "I will just put my name up for local office and see where I get," the odds would be impossibly long that he could ever have reached the heights he did. He knew that there were hundreds of local politicians elected in Massachusetts alone, but only two U.S. Senators from that State and only one President. So why in the world spend more time than necessary in the crowded lower ranks?

When **Jeb Bush**, Governor of Florida, decided to run for office, he did not run first for the Legislature, for Congress, or Mayor. He went right for the top. I asked what he was thinking when he made that decision. He explained:

> *Because I thought I could make a difference more in that job and it was an executive job, which fits my personality more perhaps. I mean, I guess to put into perspective, you know I'm in my 7th year starting in January, a lot of people probably want me to run for the next U.S. Senate opening. That would be if I was thinking about this like a career. That would be the next job open, would an open Senate seat. But I have no interest. I don't have the temperament or maybe I'm too impatient, but I think the executive office is where you can really make a difference. You can set the agenda and you can carry it out, and we've done a lot as a team up there in Tallahassee, but it matters who is in the executive position a lot. I've learned it's not so much what your beliefs are in any way; it's your ability to take the heat and absorb the blows and to stay the course and not worry about what everybody else thinks.*

This lesson, which I knew intuitively early in life, I was surprised to learn had been recognized and articulated long ago. Edward Bok, a Pulitzer Prize winning author for his autobiography, told of his life coming to America in the second half of the 1800s, and rising to the top of journalism and business with the Ladies' Home Journal. He wrote: "He looked at the top, and instead of finding it overcrowded, he was surprised at the few who had reached there; the top fairly begged for more to climb to its heights."[13] He knew, though, that that space at the top was not to be filled by the nine to five workers who would not put in the extra effort and devote the extra time. Yet, I am convinced that **the additional time and effort are incrementally small**, and success at reaching the top actually starts with realizing that you want to be there, that you deserve to be there, and that the option of being there is open to you.

When asked in an interview on CBS's *60 Minutes* if he would like to run for President, California Governor Arnold Schwarzenegger said, "I think...why not? I mean, anyone with my way of thinking you always shoot for the top." He has not done bad shooting, considering he has reached number one in the world in body building; and then decided to enter acting, and reached number one in the world in salary for an actor and box office receipts for his movies; then he decided to go into politics and reached the number one job available to anyone not born in the United States, Governor of the largest State in the Country.

Of course, in setting your sights on the top, you cannot lose sight of the here and now. Wanting the top job without putting your all into today's job is folly. The most successful people never lose sight of how important it is to do your best and give your full effort all the time.

Madeleine Albright, former Secretary of State:

I think that people have to understand that you have to pay your dues. I've paid my dues. I worked very hard in a whole host of other things that took me a long time. I got paid back pretty well, but I really do think that it's just this kind of sense that nobody owes you a living, nobody owes you a job.... I also think that often people who get something too easily in the beginning don't know quite why. Some of it isn't just raw talent, some of it has to, you never know...but then they get disappointed when it doesn't last. It's a lot easier to work your way up, than to be up and then go down, and so I think the time is worth it....If you start at the top, it's a little harder to get real satisfaction out of how you got there. And part of success, to go back to your original question, part of success is having gotten there.

Clarence Otis, CEO, Darden Restaurants:

I've always felt like, let's do an outstanding job here and see what materializes. What I do believe, if you do a great job in an organization that is successful, then there should be a next level, and it's very hard to predict what that's going to be because things move around. I think you need to be open to any number of possibilities. So when the Smokey Bones opportunity came to me, to move out of finance and into a leadership role in general management of a restaurant company, that wasn't a goal I had set. But I thought about it and thought it would be pretty interesting. It was a great business from my perspective, for a lot of reasons, and so I did that.

Susan Story, CEO, Gulf Power Co.:

It's not that everything I did every day was to move me to the top. Because I really do believe that number one, you need to be outstanding where you are currently, and for people to know what you are doing. And then it takes care of itself; it really does. As opposed to someone who, as soon as they get, and I've known people like this, as soon as they get one job, all they're focused on is their next job. I think they're very ineffective because of it.

Nina Tassler, President, CBS Entertainment:

I am very comfortable doing what I do, and I was very comfortable doing drama....I literally kind of kept my head down and just went about my business. Each time a promotion came up, it wasn't anything I sought. It was always a surprise. I mean there was never a step along the way where I said, "I want this, you know I going to go get x." I just wanted to do the best job I possibly can and let whatever happens happen. We were on vacation last August, when my boss got promoted to Co-President of Viacom. We knew that there were going to be a lot of changes internally at the network but nobody really knew what was going to happen. But I was still totally focused on just doing what I do. I got a call, my boss said, "we decided we want you to be President of the Network." I almost had a stroke. It just never entered my—I mean I still have trouble reconciling that. You know, you can't really worry about how much money you make, because there'll always be someone down the hall who makes more money than you do. Once you sort of let that go and adopt that mentality of doing the best job you possibly can and let that satisfaction come from the quality of the work—everything gets a lot easier. I just never expected that. Ironically, what I was kind of thinking about was—I love production and I love having worked at a studio for 8 years when Paramount became one of the Viacom properties. I thought, 'you know, this would be great to run the television Division.' That's actually what I was thinking about.

Certainly there are natural advantages that some people have which others do not. Studies have shown that tall people do better (and better in this context means hired sooner, paid more, more admired, more frequently elected) than short people; slim people do better than fat people; white people do better than minorities; men do better than women. A lot of this is the product of prejudice, but that makes it no less a reality when we set out to take on the world. But much of these **inherent advantages are easily overcome by factors that** *are* **in our control:** Well-spoken people will do better than those who are not articulate; outgoing people will do better than quiet, shy people; well-read people will do better than those who are not; neatly groomed and professionally dressed people will do better than sloppily groomed or carelessly dressed people. You can control how much you know, how friendly you are, how much knowledge you acquire, how well you dress, how firm your handshake. So make the choice; take the time and make the effort to look and sound your best...all the time.

Never Undervalue Yourself

When my partner and I began our practice of law in January, 1973, we got off to a pretty good start. We were not yet making a lot of money, but we were gaining a reputation in our field of practice and our community. Clients were coming in at a steady pace and we were busy. Our fee at that time was typically $25 an hour. At a certain point, in 1974, we were so busy, we were telling clients we could accept their case but could not get to it for two months. That did not deter them, and the in-flow of clients continued.

I had an idea! I went to my partner and said, "Right now we are charging $25 an hour and have more work than we can handle. Let's raise our fees to $50 an hour. We will have half the clients and make the same money."

My partner, Gary, was not sure. "What if we do that and lose a lot more than half our clients?" he asked. I said that while there was that risk, I did not think it would happen and we should give it a try. With some trepidation, he agreed. Overnight we doubled our hourly rate. Overnight our business *doubled*.

There are a couple of lessons in this experience. First, I learned that no one wants a cheap lawyer. People believe that if something costs more, it is worth more. Second, I learned that **people will place on you the value you place on yourself.** It is for this reason that it is important that you never undervalue yourself.

At various times in our lives and careers we have to decide if we will be "easy to get" or "hard to get". Is there any among us who does not believe that the person or objective that is "hard to get," is more worth acquiring or achieving? Bridget Jones gets the guy in the movie, but in real life, if someone thinks so little of him or her self, they rarely end up with the person or position they might desperately want. You have to **start with the right belief system.** You must believe that you are worth that person's attention, you are worth being selected for that position, you are worth the price you charge for your goods or service.

When you believe in yourself, there is then a magical transformation of what other people believe. They will tend to believe of you what you believe of yourself. Your own self-confidence becomes contagious. But you might say, "I am not self confident." Then I suggest you fake it. Pretty soon you will believe it, too.

Market Your Brand

When my younger daughter began college with an acting career in mind, I suggested that she take a course in Public Relations and a course in marketing. Why? Because **marketing is involved in everything** you do. I had told her earlier on, that it is not enough to have talent. There are a lot of talented people singing in a bar in Maine. Putting aside the unique or extraordinary talents that come along rarely to the truly special few, talent is not often the distinguishing factor between those who make it and those who do not. More often than not, marketing is.

In his book, *Rich Dad, Poor Dad*, Robert Kiyosaki tells the story of a young reporter who was interviewing him for a story. After taking her notes for the story, the reporter told Kiyosaki that she was an aspiring author and asked if he could share with her some advice. He suggested she take a course on sales. The reporter was offended. She objected that she had a Masters Degree in Literature and it was demeaning for him to suggest that the key to her getting her work published was to take a course of sales. Kiyosaki told her to look at her notes: "You described me as 'best selling author,' not 'best writing author.'"

It is very nice if you can be the best at what you do, writing, acting, retailing, accounting, whatever. Certainly it is desirable to strive for that. Most often, though, the determination of who is "best" is subjective— there are no tests which quantify which lawyer writes the best contract, or gives the best business advice. Which singer is best depends on the ear of the beholder. Moreover, the buying public is not really in a position to evaluate the relative quality of those in most fields of endeavor. They rely on what they are conditioned to believe (e.g. you charge more, so you are probably better) or what they are told (word of mouth recommendations) or what they read (articles, etc. describing your achievements and ability). You would probably agree with me that while Madonna is not the best singer in the world, she is the mother of invention and reinvention, a genius at marketing. While your impact on your natural talents may be limited, your impact on how you are perceived is not.

Particularly when you are dealing with intangible attributes (i.e. those that we cannot readily determine through the senses), **managing perception** becomes even more important. Harry Beckwith has written several books on this subject directed to those who are marketing services, including *Selling the Invisible* and *What Clients Love*. In the latter book, he argues that "we have the experiences we expect to have, based on our perceptions that preceded those experiences." This is really another way of saying that people will react to us in the way we prepare them, though our own conduct, our appearance, our expectations and even our own self-perception, to react to us.

Tom Peters, the co-author of the groundbreaking business book *"In Search of Excellence"* written in 1980, and author of many others (including the one I enjoyed most, *Thriving on Chaos*), wrote a quirky little book in the mid 90's called *The Brand You*. In it, he posits that each of us has the potential to make ourselves into a brand. To understand this, we need some definitions.

Marketing starts with Positioning. Positioning refers to **the *position* a person or product occupies in the mind of the consuming public.** Every person with a service to sell and every product for sale, wants to occupy a position in the mind of the potential buyer. In effect, it is **a promise of the uniqueness of that person or product.** In terms of people, it means: what do you stand for? What is the promise that someone meeting you or buying your services anticipates? Let's take writers, for example. If we hear the name Stephen King, we do not expect a romance novel or a historical action novel. We expect to get the best of horror with a supernatural twist and turn. Because Stephen King *consistently fulfills that promise*, he has become a BRAND.

The same is true of writings themselves. Many people have read *Chicken Soup for the Soul*. Even though most could probably not name the authors, they know the book offers uncomplicated, inspirational guidance for self-improvement. The consistent delivery on the promise allows the authors to follow up with a series such as *Chicken Soup for a Mother's Soul*, *Chicken Soup for the Teenage Soul*, etc. With 100 million copies sold, they must be doing something right. And the 34 publishers who turned them down before they found an obscure publisher to take them on, have to be feeling pretty stupid. Here is another example of the importance of never giving up. Don't be deterred by conventional wisdom since it is usually...conventional.

Likewise, *Don't Sweat the Small Stuff*. On its heels comes *Don't Sweat the Small Stuff at Work*, *Don't Sweat the Small Stuff in Relationships*, etc. Another example is the "___ *for Dummies*" series. These titles have created a Brand for themselves, and **brands enhance value**. In the case of many products, the entire value is found in the brand. In other words, there is no real difference between gasoline bought at the pump, but because we have been conditioned to believe the value propositions of Shell, or BP, or Amoco, we consistently prefer one brand over the others.

Alan Potamkin and his brother own a vast nationwide empire of car dealerships (with sales over $1.2 *billion* annually), real estate, and, until recently, media properties (TV and radio stations). A few years ago, Alan told me that the best book he had read on marketing was a tiny book written by Jack Trout and Al Ries called *The 22 Immutable Laws of Marketing*. Considering the source, I went out and bought it. The book proves that good things come in small packages (just as for those looking to improve their writing skills, the same can be said of *The Elements of Style* by Strunk and White). Both Trout and Ries have gone on to write a number of excellent books, separately, but to anyone looking for ideas on how to market themselves or their products, I can recommend their joint effort as a good starting point.

Clearly, the greatest advantage in brand creation and in the achievement of success goes to the people who are "originals". **Those**

who are the first in a category will always stand out. The more narrowly you define the category, the easier it is to be first (or failing at first, be second, or failing in that, be first in the opposite category). Even if you are in a crowded category, you should always look for a way to stand out, to position yourself as the first or best of something, and find a way to spread the word. You want to stand for something. The originals always do best in a crowded field, and this is true of products (we usually call a facial tissue a Kleenex because it was the original or ask for a Coke rather than a cola) and of people. **You are a brand, and you should always market your brand.**

How to do this can fill at least another full book (or several), such as the ones recommended above, so I will not go into detail here. Suffice to say that the opportunities are many. They include writing articles, giving speeches, meeting the right people in the press and keeping them properly informed. Joining the right organizations with affinity based on common profession or common interests is also valuable. Joining an organization is, in and of itself, usually meaningless. You have to devote the time to be active in the organization to get maximum value out of your membership. You must develop relationships and demonstrate that you are worthy of trust. **Don't be bashful. If you have a story to tell, tell it. In fact, if you don't have a story to tell, create one, then tell it.**

By creating a story, I am not suggesting you lie. I am suggesting that you apply a little imagination and ingenuity to figure out the best way to get the idea across to others. In 1987, my wife opened a showroom in Florida featuring a well-known brand in china, glassware, and furniture: Rosenthal. Rosenthal is a century old German company known for its fine products that combine the highest elements of contemporary design (form) and function. At the grand opening of her business, Philip Rosenthal, then in his 70's, came from Germany to lend his celebrity to the event. He noticed that some of the crystal glasses did not have nameplates in front of them describing the design and the artist who had designed it. At lunch, he said it was important to put up those little nameplates with the descriptions. He held up a water glass and said: "Without a story, this is just a glass." His point was, it is the story that conveys the unique attributes to the public and justifies the higher price. That is no less true of people.

Staying on Top

Perhaps even harder than getting to the top, is staying there. People who achieve great things can find that it is too easy to slip down the slope from the mountaintop. Often, having put in the enormous effort and perseverance to accomplish great goals, we can become complacent. Nothing stands still. **Change is constant.** If you do not continue working at success once having achieved it, it will slip away.

There are some pretty obvious reasons for this. For one, competition always increases. For years, no one thought it possible to run a four minute mile. Then one day, somebody did. That first time was the result of years of training and grueling effort, of a grand dream and enormous amounts of sweat. Once that mark was broken, though, it was then beaten by other people, over and over again. The record for a one mile run kept getting faster and faster. Olympic world records are set and broken by hundredths of a second. Once you can produce a product cheaper than anyone else, somebody else will find a way to produce it cheaper than you can. Once you can fly a plane higher and faster, someone will soon find a way to fly one even higher and even faster. If you stop to rest on your laurels, you will soon be passed by.

It is also possible to fall from grace by taking yourself and your accomplishments too seriously. It is important to **maintain a sense of humor.** People who are cheerful and have a sense of humor about themselves, their accomplishments, and the world at large, find that other people root for them and share in the joy of their success. People who take themselves too seriously, who are humorless, find that the world will rejoice in their defeat and find ways to assist their decline. A related concept is expressed in the old saying, "Be nice to people on your way up. You will meet them again on your way down." I have known people who have reached the heights in their field, only to fall, as is often the case, on difficult times. How they were able to handle the difficulties usually depended, on the good will—or lack thereof—that they had accumulated on the way up.

Here are two examples I can call "A Tale of Two Politicians." One friend had been a powerful Senator and County Commissioner. He was widely anticipated to be the next Mayor of Miami-Dade County. He was blindsided by accusations from some criminal elements that he had been involved in a drug and sex scandal. The scandal got daily headlines, while the FBI proof that these charges were false, including a drug test he volunteered to take, was barely mentioned. His political enemies came out of every nook and cranny. Before long, he narrowly lost re-election and left under a dark cloud to start a new life in another country. What had happened? I have my theory. He was a brilliant guy who understood and could manipulate the system, could make things happen in Government. For all his ability and power, he was not well liked. Most of his friends were friends because of what he could do for or to them. His enemies kept quiet while he was on top because he could be vengeful. For no particular reason, he could lash out at people or be dismissive. And everyone took it. Once he ran into a problem, even those who knew the charges were false, stood back and watched his slide with barely concealed glee.

Compare this to another friend who was a highly effective and well—regarded U.S. Congressman who got in trouble because he had not reported some income for tax purposes. He was forced to resign, and even served a couple of months in a Federal correctional institution. He came out without his old power, with no source of income or prospect for any, disbarred because of the conviction and unable to practice law, feeling terrible sense of shame and loss. Within a very short time he was making a good living and reintegrated into the halls of power as a successful lobbyist. What was the difference? During his ascendancy to fame and power, he stayed friends with those who had been friends before and treated all the people he met with proper dignity and respect. When he hit hard times, people felt badly for him and went out of their way to help, often with projects for him to work on and make money. He is also a good example of perseverance, because he did not come out from prison and hide away. Difficult as it undoubtedly was, he forced himself to keep on going, to get out in the community at charitable and political events, to become involved and stay in touch with all his old friends and contacts. This is a double testament: to being good to people on the way up, and to never giving up. There is also a message there about adaptability to change.

The colloquial expression for what I am suggesting is that one should not "get too big for your britches". (It has been a long time since anyone wore britches, so the expression has lost much of its currency.) There is a more modern song by Chris Rea called "God's Great Banana Skin" in which he is really talking about not taking things for granted and not thinking you are better than everyone else or that you know more than everyone else. I find that too often extremely smart people make the big mistake of thinking everyone else is stupid. This attitude, which they are typically unable to conceal, results in misguided attempts to manipulate others, and does not win them friends or allies.

Those who reach the top and those who stay there understand, at least at some level, **the importance of networking**. By this, I am referring simply to the **systematic meeting of people and staying in touch with them.**

Jorge de Cespedes, President of PharMed, gave good examples of how this helps in business :

> *{M}y wife often tells me, "you never stop selling". It's a lifestyle. One of the guys at PharMed that we hired a couple of years ago really put us on the map because he was a major league player. He had decided late in his career, by his own choice, that he liked enough of what we were doing here that he was going to give up his nice cushy job, with a big health company to come work with a company like ours. People in the industry noticed him come to work with us and said "wow this company must really be something, that they would attract this kind of talent".*

> *I think that's what he wanted. He wanted to be part of something that he could help create. That he could help mold and he did. He retired a couple years ago at age 67 after spending the last 10 years of his career with us. But he used to talk about being successful in this industry and how to make it a lifestyle. In our particular industry where we deal mostly with hospitals, it's not just good enough to know the president of the hospital or the director of purchasing. You have to know everybody and you have to know the wives' names or the kids' names and what are their hobbies and what are sporting events and the more you are in that mind set, the more success you are going to find.*

The more you get to know people, the more success you will find. But getting to know them means really knowing them: what they like and dislike, need or want, what is happening in their lives. The more you engage people, the stronger your relationships. The stronger your relationships, the more certain will be your success.

People appreciate small acts of kindness, and they appreciate being remembered. If you see an article that someone you know might find interesting (even if it is likely they would have seen it on their own), cut it out and send it to the person with a little hand written note: "thought you would find this interesting." Remember special events and send a note on occasions like birthdays.[14] Of course, a congratulatory note when something good happens is always appreciated. Even more so, an expression of concern when something bad happens.

When I was a former Legislator running for higher office, U.S. Congress, I beat the incumbent Congressman in a Democratic primary. The phone rang off the hook. Everyone in the world, it seemed, called to congratulate me and remind me they had supported me and were my friends. I got many such notes as well. A few weeks later, I lost the General Election to the Republican candidate. Silence. No phone calls. No notes. Nada. I am sure that part of it is that people simply don't know what to say, but you do remember those who call. Likewise, it is easy to call someone and congratulate them on the birth of a child (and desirable to do so) but it is much more difficult to call and offer condolences on the death of a loved one. In truth, there really is nothing helpful to say other than that you are sorry. The call, however, does a world of good and will be greatly appreciated.

So, part of your marketing effort in reaching the top, and part of defending your brand to stay on top, is networking. Meet people. Keep track of them. Stay in touch with them. **Be a source of support** when they need it. It vastly increases the odds that they will be there for you when you need it, and will help you on your journey to the top.

Having reached the top, look higher. Always be open to change because, like it or not, change is a-coming. Embrace it. And find ways to reinvent yourself and what you do. If you are not in charge of the change, then someone else will profit from it at your expense.

REFLECTIONS AND APPLICATIONS—CHAPTER 9

1. Select a "Brand Name" for your self. Does it describe your abilities and aspirations?
2. How would you describe the unique interests or attributes that you possess which distinguish you in a positive way?

CHAPTER 10
THE SEVENTH SECRET: POWER ABHORS A VACUUM

Anyone who has taken a course in high school physics has heard that "nature abhors a vacuum." You have seen the teacher suck the air out of a bottle, creating a vacuum, and then seen how any nearby object is sucked into that vacuum. If there is a vacuum, nature wants to fill it. I have found that the same is true with power.

As I mentioned earlier, in 1990 my partner, Jeff, became a judge and left our law practice. Jeff had been in charge of a major department of our law firm, commercial litigation. When he left, a junior partner, Allen Levine, began to guide the other lawyers in that department, hand out assignments, review their work. No one had appointed Allen to do this. He recognized that there was a void and simply stepped up to fill it. A few months later, he said to me, "A few years ago when I started working here you told me something I didn't understand, but I get it now." "What," I asked, "was that?" Allen replied: "You told me 'power abhors a vacuum.' I now get it." And get it he did. What had begun as Allen filling a vacuum and assuming a leadership role, was later formalized.

What Allen came to learn was that a critical element in achieving success is seizing opportunities that present themselves. Neither we nor he could have predicted that his department of the law firm would become leaderless. When it did, he could have waited for us to appoint a new head of the department. Instead, he saw a job that needed doing, so he did it. By assuming the responsibility, he made the job his. The lesson is that if you stand around waiting for the call, it may never come.

Susan Story, CEO of Gulf Power Co. is another great example of someone who understands this. She told me:

As I started my career, of course growing up the way I did in a rural Alabama town, I didn't know what a president of a company was or a CEO of a company was. I started as an engineer in a nuclear power plant and just believed in working as hard as I could and doing the best job I could because that's the way I had been raised. I started progressing pretty rapidly through managerial ranks and, interestingly, never really looked at what the next job would be. It was more of creating something in the job I was in that had not been there before. I went into a lot of jobs that would have job descriptions, but never really took that "as this is what I need to do". Success to me was what is out there that is not being done that I can do? It's: someone's not doing this, regardless of who is supposed to be responsible. Let me go, if you don't care who gets the credit—go and do it and I started being noticed for it. Also I think communication skills are very important, being good on your feet and talking to people. So I just kind of kept progressing through ranks. When people would say, "why are you successful," I guess my bottom line answer would be just that I enjoy I everything I do, I put everything I've got into it, and I want to be part of the team that does great things.

If you take the initiative and fill the void that needs filling, you create ownership of the territory. You step up, do the job, and more often than not it becomes yours; you will own it.

Is there an element of risk in taking such a bold approach? Of course there is, but **few things worthwhile are ever accomplished without risk.** The most successful people all know that there are risks they must face to get ahead. **Jorge de Cespedes** believes that risk taking is at the core of being successful in business:

Actually to this day I believe this very strongly that entrepreneurs are born entrepreneurs. They are not made. You know, you can't make yourself be an entrepreneur. It is a certain personality set that goes along with a certain risk taking, not being afraid to fail. Most people live their lives, in my opinion, not so much seeking success, but staying away from risk. There's a mind set, I relate a lot of things to sports...show me football. If you have a 10 point lead, why do so many teams stop trying? [They] play it safe and very often lose.... You know you have to accept failure once in a while.

When **Clarence Otis** gave up a secure and lucrative position in investment banking to enter the restaurant business, he knew he was taking a risk:

*I'd say it was, but **I felt comfortable taking a risk**. I knew the financial community well enough that you could always go back—I felt like I like I could always go back and do that. I liked Chemical Bank and the whole culture, so there was the risk of leaving a place that I really liked and where I was well liked. But I thought it was worth doing. The opportunity I saw with Darden was that it was in an industry that still had a lot of growth. It's market is in casual dining and Darden clearly had everything it took to continue to lead the industry. And so, as it grew it could be significant.*

And risk is the very essence of **Nina Tassler**'s professional life at CBS:

*I think that **much of our business is predicated on the reality that there will be failure, and you cannot let that influence your desire to take risks**. There's a seasonal structure to our business and every year we sort of reinvent ourselves and, I think that when you have a creative drive, when you have a vision for something, when you are a part of a collective creative division, (and working in a network you are part of a very big organization within which there are many different creative divisions)…it's a communications business, so you have to communicate, you have to find a way to express ideas and to be a facilitator for producers and artists and writers and actors and directors to communicate their ideas. You can find yourself settling and find yourself basically mired in the business aspect of it, as opposed to really going out on a limb, taking chances and really doing what you are supposed to do in network television, which is to set out to communicate creative ideas to the broadest segment of the population.*

These successful people know, that there is no advancement without risk, but they understand that the upside is worth it. They are not unaware, perhaps not even unafraid, but they push ahead bravely to make their mark in life and career, to be a success and to feel like one. As Robert Kriegel said in his book, *If it ain't broke…Break It*:

[W]e must continually change our thinking and behavior. Taking risks is a necessity, there is no other choice. Playing it safe is dangerous and futile, and the notion of a comfort zone is illusory. There is no safe harbor from this storm to survive, much less succeed, you must learn to be out in front of the wave.... [M]odern life guarantees nothing but change and...if we aren't taking risks and in constant motion, we will neither adapt, nor prosper. It is not surprising to find this advice coming consistently from top performers in many fields. The biggest risk is not to risk.

So, when an opportunity presents itself, step on up and take it. Don't wait for an invitation. Most people think you need luck to be a success, and that is probably true. But the best definition of luck is that I first heard from philosopher Stanford Paul: **Luck is when opportunity meets preparation.**

What he means by that is this: You may be well prepared, but if the opportunity never presents itself to apply what you know, you will not achieve your objective. The opportunity of a lifetime may present itself, but if you are not well prepared, you may not be positioned to seize the opportunity, or you might not even recognize it.

Jorge de Cespedes told me: "**The harder you work, the luckier you get.** There is no doubt." **Wayne Huizenga's** big break "came up at lunch one day and actually it was being in the right place and the right time and **taking advantage of an opportunity**...... [O]nce you fall into the opportunity, you have to take advantage of it and make something happen.." Was Wayne lucky with Waste Management and Blockbuster and AutoNation and the rest? He thinks so: "I think the common theme there, it's just having been lucky and having the ability to have the right people to make it happen." But clearly his luck was convergence of preparation and opportunity, allowing him to recognize and take advantage of the opportunities when they came along. **Clarence Otis,** too, understands taking advantage of an opportunity. He cautioned,

> *I think you have to be open to sort of planning things as they come. I don't know that you help yourself by doing too much planning, because if you're planning and something comes along that doesn't fit the plan, you may walk past it even though that's the right opportunity.*

Likewise, novelist **Brad Meltzer,** reflecting on how much of his success is preparation and how much is opportunity, concluded,

> *It is where the two meet. There is no doubt about it. There are people who are fantastically talented and never get a shot, and that's just a fact. It's a fact in every business which is why, whenever I see these people who think that they are the top of the world and they are the greatest, I'm always thinking: you got lucky that someone said yes. That's it, and if you forget that for a moment, you are going to be one of those obnoxious jackasses and, you know, I think **so much of it depends on being in that right place at the right time. My agent once said to me it takes one person to say yes. All our job is, is to find that one person.***

As I have pointed out above, we each have some ability to create opportunities; but we all have the ability (and, I would submit, the obligation) to be prepared. Part of preparation is setting goals and planning to achieve the goals. Part of it is making sure you read and learn the things which will be useful in the future. It means taking the steps to read about, study, emulate and, if possible, meet the people who have achieved success in the arena in which you want to play. Help make your luck by being sure you are prepared. If you want to be a lawyer, be the best lawyer you can be. That means more than studying what they teach in law school. It means seeking out and studying the best lawyers in your chosen field and learning what they do and how they do it. It means practicing those lessons and the techniques until you have mastered them. The same rules apply if you want to be a great engineer or great doctor or great journalist or great singer or great teacher (and I do hope whatever field you decide to enter you will do it with the intention to be great).

Curiosity is essential to full preparation. Billionaire and best-selling author Donald Trump says, "I've never met a successful person who wasn't curious. [You should] ask a lot of questions." Brian Tracy teaches that the best selling "technique" is to ask a lot of questions. Success comes to those who ask questions, who listen, who learn...a lot faster than it comes to those who are compelled always to talk. The super-successful people I spoke with certainly agree.

Jeb Bush, Governor of Florida:

There is stuff that I don't know still about the details of some policy. I *guess **the thing I've learned to do is not be embarrassed about*** ***asking stupid questions.** You know what I mean? Stupid questions* *are typically the ones…a lot of times people don't speak plain spoken* *English. Little acronyms, we've fought a lonely battle against acronyms,* *losing it. But **I ask people to speak in plain English. I ask them*** ***to, if I really don't understand it, I make them pause and*** ***tell it to me in English.** It helps a lot in government meetings, they* *are always double the number of people as in private meetings. There's* *a big room with a lot of people and some guy, smartie pants, will start* *talking about something he thinks maybe he knows more about than* *everybody in the room. No one will want to say, "well wait a second,* *can you explain this to me again and there is always a <u>sigh</u> of relief* *when I do it because I'm not worried about what people think, I guess.* *So I ask a lot of questions, because it's the best way to learn and in* *many cases I end up having to make a decision. I ask a ton of questions* *and it helps me understand. And then the other thing is, we have a* *culture in my office where the youngest analyst in the budget office is* *free to speak their mind. And there is a fun part of my job which is* *when the Legislature finishes; it's always fun when their session's over.* *There's 500 bills that pass, typically, you've got some of the stupidest* *bills, littlest tiniest little things and some very large things and it's* *never black and white. I mean on the tough ones, there's provisions in* *the Bill that would be a poison Pill or then you have to go through* *the rest of the Bill and it's good. Do I accept this? This was wrong to* *put it in there, it was probably for some economic gain for a very small* *group of people or creating a barrier of entry for others, you know, using* *the political process for the wrong reasons. And then you are confronted* *with a challenge and haunted. Sometimes there are moral questions* *involved, or it's pretty petty stuff, I mean for me at least. I take my* *job seriously and I want to try and be consistent. We'll have meetings* *where there are 30 people in the room and I will ask everyone of them* *to give me their opinion and what it does first of all, it helps them* *understand my job, which is a little different from theirs. It puts them* *in the position where they say yes, no, rather than well on the other* *hand…which is what advisors, counselors do. Leaders have to say* *"yes" or they have to say "no" and it's incredibly interesting, the added value I get from listening to other people's opinions on really difficult matters. So I listen a lot and I ask question, and I listen.*

Clarence Otis, CEO, Darden Restaurants:

I think the key to business for me has been just having curiosity and so just trying to understand the organization that you're in, trying to understand other organizations that are doing the same things or other organizations that have the same challenges, and how have they were handled, how the folks that have been successful or how the people have not been successful handled them? In doing that at every level. So even as an entry level. It's not that you have a chance to affect the direction of the company, but you want to understand what the organization is trying to accomplish? You want to get a feel for how good a job are we doing? So the liberal arts orientation of really being curious and following that curiosity and satisfying it has been a huge help in business….

I think you really do need to be curious about, the world around you. You need to be curious about the people that you meet. You know, who is this person? Why are they the way they are? What it is about them culturally? What is it about them personally that makes them that way? You will learn more about yourself. You need to be curious about the way you are and the place that you are. What is this place? How did it come to be the way it is and the people here the way they are? How do they differ from how people behave elsewhere? So I think the curiosity thesis is very important.

Part of the preparation for success may be career specific, such as the proper education for the field you have chosen. Part of it is in the development of habits such as those described in the earlier chapters, which help you recognize and seize upon opportunities and give you the tools to succeed. Some are of a more general nature that will help you have the basic knowledge necessary to simply travel in the circles of people who can help you advance your goals. For example, I always suggest to young people that in addition to being well-read in general, it is important to stay current. You want to be able to walk into almost any room and be able to converse reasonably intelligently with just about anyone, on subjects of interest **to them**. If you need a hint at what will interest them, be observant. See what they wear, how they furnish their office, what photos (their kids or the Swiss Alps or their dogs, etc) adorn their walls, and what art work. If you know your dog breeds, exotic locations, styles of art and artists, you will not only pick up on their interests but be able to break the ice by conversing about them.

The key to developing and maintaining this important general knowledge of the world around you, is to expose yourself to it. I advise reading a weekly news magazine such as *Time Magazine* or *Newsweek*. But you must read it cover to cover. Yes, read the national and international political and economic stories. However, you should also read the stories about art and music and science and the book reviews. You would be amazed at how far those little bits of information will get you. I personally read *Time* each week, *Forbes* (a business magazine) bi-weekly, and *Florida Trend Magazine* (a Florida focused business and public policy magazine) monthly. I also read other randomly selected magazines, and my daily newspaper. It is vital to read the newspaper. I always tell young people that if they don't have a lot of time in the morning they can skim over the national and international news—you will hear it several times that day on the radio, on TV or see it on CNN or other news web sites. You can also skim the sports page if you care about those things. It makes for decent water cooler conversation. Better, though, to read the local news section and the business section. That is where you will most likely find the news that will be most useful to you in your career objectives. I occasionally get the objection that many people who read these things quickly forget what they have read. You do not need a photographic memory. You need only get in the habit of reading these sources regularly, and soon you will find that the topics repeat and you are gradually absorbing much of the knowledge.

We have all known or heard of people who were an overnight success. More often than not, they were an overnight success after twenty years of hard work. You just never learned of or observed the preparation that went into it. In reality, such seemingly overnight success is akin to the results (in political change, social change, marketing phenomena, and even epidemic disease) described by Malcolm Gladwell in his book, *The Tipping Point*. He theorizes and demonstrates that many changes which seem to come upon an individual, a company, a society or a body politic, virtually spontaneously, are not spontaneous at all. In fact, they are the result of the gradual and imperceptible forces that build and build until they suddenly "tip" over the metaphorical edge, become ubiquitous, and appear obvious to one and all. Gosh, it just seemed to happen overnight. But it did not.

I have known too many people who are looking for the quick score, the fast money, a shortcut to fame or riches. This is almost always the attitude of failure. Surely, there is the occasional genuine overnight success. There is, after all, the role of genuine luck. But far more often, such an attitude, the search for the shortcut, is a guaranty of simply a shortcut to oblivion. Only one out of 13 million of us will win on this week's Florida lottery ticket. Not the odds to plan your life on. The surer path to success is the consistent motion forward, building on what you learned or did before, taking those **incremental small steps**. Well-planned, meticulously executed small steps—in other words, preparation—are the way to enduring success.

Being prepared brings us back full circle to focus. It often requires hard work and discipline. Encountering opportunity brings us back to goal setting and a relaxed attitude that will allow us to be open to seeing the opportunity when either it presents itself or you create it. But when the two come together: preparation and opportunity, the chemical reaction is explosive, and usually in a very positive way. In the example of my partner, Allen, who stepped up to fill a power void in the leadership of our law firm, the opportunity was there by chance. However, he was astute enough to recognize it, and well prepared to take advantage of it. He had honed his legal skills and studied what his predecessor had done, so that he felt confident he could step in when the moment arrived. A power vacuum wants to be filled, but it must be something (or someone) with real substance that fills it.

REFLECTIONS AND APPLICATIONS—CHAPTER 10

1. Are you ready to give yourself fully to the pursuit of success?
2. Have you started yet? (If you have not, why not? You may find the sacrifices exhilarating!!)

CHAPTER 11
THE EIGHTH SECRET:THE PATHS OF LIFE

O K. Here is the part where I go spiritual on you. Stay with me, though.

I truly believe that for each of us **there is a pre-determined path** which we are destined to follow. If we do follow that path, we will find purpose, fulfillment, and success waiting at the end of the journey. The trouble, if it is indeed trouble, is that **we all have free will.** The path laid out for us to reach our destiny is full of detours and branches. At any point along the way we can veer from the intended path. We can go wrong; we can go very wrong.

The good news is that each branch from the path, in turn, branches many more times. Along the way there is always a branch that will afford the opportunity to find our way back to the intended path. Sometimes this can happen sooner, sometimes later, and sometimes not at all. The latter category, which is, alas, fairly large, belongs to those who do not find enduring happiness or success.

Some people may see this construct as a sort of divine plan. They think of it as God's plan. If things go well, they thank God (there is certainly no harm and plenty of good in expressing gratitude). If things go poorly, they accept or deride the result as God's will. But I do not believe in a benevolent God who will take the time to make sure I follow the proper path to my destiny. Nor do I believe in a vengeful God who will punish me for transgressions and steer me down the wrong branch when I reach a crossroad. The choices were and always remain mine, which way to go.

Jeb Bush, Governor of Florida:

> *I think God has a plan for all of us. I don't think it's preordained, I don't think it is. I think we have a say in our destiny, but it's God's hands on all of us and my faith really gives me serenity more than anything else. A clearer*

head. It's a way to filter out a lot of the things that make life much more complicated than it needs to be. Which is why I am thankful to God to have a love for him and a relationship, but I don't think we're plankton, you know. I think we're just not here to respond to heat and light. I do think we have the ability to shape our future. It can be guided by different things. It can be guided by...your faith guides you hopefully with primary religions and at least not the ones on the margins. It will guide you to be more humble and selfless and have courage, and it will guide you to adhere to basic virtues. If you don't have it, you can still achieve that. I'm not saying that people without faith can't adhere to a virtuous life. It can be good, different, and I don't how they do it, but I know they don't have a relationship with God and they look like they are doing pretty good.

Brad Meltzer, novelist:

*I just feel like **I've had too many things that I've been fortunate enough to stumble into to, not believe that there is some grand plan.** Of course you have to [recognize them when they cross your path]. You can't just walk past them, but at the same time they still have to cross your path and some people will call whatever.... I think I do believe God is definitely with me on that level. Has put all these different things in front of me to trip over, and maybe I'm just stupid enough that I keep falling, but I really just don't think it's just my, my wonderful brain and my fantastic imagination that's got me do the things I've been able to do.*

Clarence Otis, CEO, Darden Restaurants:

*I think it's definitely not all me. It's going to be what are the situations that you encounter and then, what are the dynamics of those situations. There are situations, **there are dynamics, that are outside your control. What's in your control is how you react to it.** There are situations and dynamics where your reaction will be, in retrospect, what you think probably was right and other cases where you think probably wasn't right, and so that's going to inform the next step on the timeline. You just have to react well more often than you don't.*

Nina Tassler, President, CBS Entertainment:

I was raised with CBS being, for most of my life, the network that we watched. I was raised on Walter Cronkite. These were shows *that I heard about. I watched Captain Kangaroo, so in truth it was the first network I was ever introduced to. In that way **I wouldn't be surprised if fate played some hand in my being at this company today. In many ways, I think that the people in my professional life,** Leslie Moonves, John Kimbell, my husband…I **have been incredibly fortunate to have been graced by very decent honest dedicated men, who valued my input and my participation, so I think that I was lucky in that my path crossed theirs, and I'm incredibly grateful for the good fortune that my family is the beneficiary of.** But I think that, like I said, fate is just a moment in time if you're not prepared for it and I think that the people who influenced me, prepared me for these moments in time.*

How then, to follow the correct path? Some times there are signs, and it merely requires being alert to them.

I remember an incident that began in law school that shaped much of my professional life. During law school I had a friend, Lou, with whom I did everything. We went to the football games together, vacationed together, went on double dates together, studied together. We took a trial practice course together in which insurance companies agreed to be bound by the results of our student trials, and required their insured customers to cooperate with us students. The class was broken up into teams of two trial lawyers on each side of each case. I assumed that Lou and I would team up but I learned that he had teamed with someone else. I then formed a team with Gary Poliakoff, who was another member of our study group.

Gary and I were assigned to represent a middle-aged man named Charles Blairney (name slightly changed to protect the innocent) who had been involved in an auto accident. We interviewed Blairney and other witnesses, investigated the scene of the accident, prepared and presented our case before a (real) judge and (student) jury. We won our case.

Four years later, I was practicing law with a group of three partners (one was my old law school buddy Lou). Gary had gone to work for his father-in-law's company. I took off three months to run for the Florida Legislature. When I returned to the office, triumphant, my three partners gathered and informed me, "We don't want a politician in our law firm."

I was pretty shocked and hurt by this and was trying to decide what to do. One thing was for sure: I was not going to dwell on it. I was going to move forward and be even more successful. I told Gary about what had happened and he said he had been thinking of practicing law as he had been trained to do, and would be interested in our going into partnership. I said I would think it over.

A few days later, I was working in my office, when the secretary announced I had a visitor. It was a Mr. Charles Blairney—the very "client" Gary and I had represented as law students several years before. After our school trial we had never seen or heard of Mr. Blairney after that. I invited him into my office. He said he had seen my sign on the door many times and today he just thought he would stop and see how I was doing as a lawyer. "By the way," he said, "what ever happened to that other fellow? You and he made great partners." He left, and I never saw him again. But I took the visit as a sign, and immediately called Gary. Thus began a partnership that has lasted 34 years. Did Charles Blairney just walk into and out of our lives at the precise moment when a path was to be chosen? What turn would my life had taken had he not walked in when he did, or if I was out of the office that day, or if he had not asked about Gary and made his comment about our working well together? I don't know. What I do know is that when I needed an answer, the answer appeared and I was receptive to it. I had reached a crossroad and the choice had become clear.

There are not always such obvious signs. Still, there is that voice within you that knows you are at a crossroad and have a path to choose; and an even quieter inner voice that will guide you in the correct direction…. if you are relaxed and open to hearing that voice. As I described in the chapter on Go With Your Gut, there are choices that should always be clear—between good and evil, right and wrong. Then there are those that are more subjective, where it not an issue of what is right and what is wrong, but rather what is right or wrong for you. Too much thought and too much logic can propel you in the wrong direction. **Intuition and instinct will be your best guides.**

Jeb Bush, Governor of Florida:

> *Decision-making is interesting where sometimes my instincts tell me it's better not to make a decision, conditions will change and the whole context of what you are looking at will change and the challenge or*

the problem goes away. But most of the time you do have to go to your core values, your principles, take the problem and have it run through. That way there is a consistency to make decisions and making them is important. People that do get paralyzed end up getting run over, like road kill.

Accepting this idea does, to some extent, require your acceptance of the notion of a higher plan. Surely, I am not the first to believe that what we can feel intuitively is as real as that which we can see and touch. Napolean Hill, in *Think and Grow Rich*, counseled the importance of being open to the "Infinite Intelligence" from which we could receive grander knowledge and vision to help us achieve our dreams.

Harvey Mackay, best selling author of *Swim With The Sharks Without Being Eaten Alive* and several other books on business and networking, wrote *We Got Fired…And It's the Best Thing That Ever Happened to Us* about successful and prominent people who found their greatest success after their biggest setbacks. In it, one chapter featured Jesse Ventura whose career as a professional wrestler, radio and TV commentator, and then, as Governor of Minnesota had its ups and downs (no pun intended). But (to continue the feeble metaphor), he always landed on his feet. Ventura told him: " Each one of us has a destiny that we're driven to by certain decisions. You may not understand why you're picking a direction in that fork in the road now, but years down the line it will come clear to you. At any given time, things happen in your life, and you haven't got a clue. I'm a great believer in fate and that things happen for a reason…." What the former wrestler, former Governor is referring to is the belief I hold and he apparently shares, that **when one door closes another will open.**

Madeleine Albright, former Secretary of State:

*The thing I think that is so important for women and men is that as we make choices about what we're going to do, I think it's important to realize that there's no one pattern. Also, **you have to be careful not to close doors as you move from one door to another, because you never know where the opportunities will come.***

Wayne Huizenga, billionaire serial entrepreneur, told me this story:

*I think, like I said, **a lot of it has been destiny**. I don't know how to describe it really, but I guess you could call it destiny. Steve*

Barrard and I have been friends for a long time. He was the CFO at Blockbuster. Then I made him the CEO at AutoNation and he did a heck of a job putting that company together, but he wasn't the right guy to manage the company and so I had to let him go. But we stayed friends. You know I mean it wasn't—he recognized it, and now he and I still remained friends the whole time. A couple of months ago he called me up and said "hey, I stumbled across a business I think we should do", and I said what's that? It's a business that operates in 42 states in the United States and 12 foreign counties, and they've got 2,000 trucks and 70,000 customers. We made the deal and now he owns 50% and I own 50%.

So, I suggested, one door had closed for Steve and another one opened. Wayne replied, "Yes, and one opened for me too."

Wayne Dyer, in his book *The Power of Intention*, teaches that, along with the importance of staying focused on what you want and maintaining a positive attitude, you should tap into "the Source". He says we must always seek to stay close to and in harmony with "Source", the energy in the universe that allows for creation, because it is through closeness to Source that we will find our intended way.

In other words, as I prefer to put it, you will find and stay on the correct path and be rewarded for having done so. The rewards may be material or may lie in the satisfaction of knowing and achieving your purpose; or it may simply be an inner peace from which you derive true happiness. Most likely, it will be some combination. Without any doubt it will make for a wonderful journey. And on that journey I wish you— Success, of course!

FOOTNOTES

[1] Wayne says people incorrectly give him credit for founding Blockbuster. He actually acquired it as an 8 store chain, and grew it to over 4,000 stores around the world. That is close enough to "founder" for me.

[2] Modern philosopher Wayne Dyer says that giving (or doing good deeds) increases seratonin levels in your brain and strengthens your immune system. Scientific studies support this notion, including various studies at Harvard's School of Public Health which demonstrate that happy, optimistic people appear to have far lower risk of disease.

[3] Apparently the same principle applies equally at the level of nations. Winston Churchill once said of General Charles de Gaulle, the post-War President of France: "England's grievous offence in de Gaulle's eyes is that she has helped France. He cannot bear to think that she needed help." Some might attribute recent French attitude towards the United States to the same offense during the same period in history.

[4] As with a marriage, a partnership is not always easy and requires some effort to make the relationship last.

[5] It sometimes seems that if you were to add up all of the six, seven, eight and nine habits, rules, secrets and laws, of happiness, success, wealth, weight loss or almost anything else, there would really be something like 1387 habits, rules, secrets and laws for you to memorize and apply. In reality, there is actually a good deal of overlap. You can study in great depth the 700+ laws of the Talmud, but you can probably get by pretty well applying the Ten Commandments. It is through constant learning, through reading and analyzing, that you will find the principles that you understand best and that work best for you.

[6] The subtitle of this book is: *How to Accomplish More by Doing Less—the Nine Essentials of 80/20 Success at Work*. Clearly they have the right number of steps (although just looking at the table of contents would give you the impression there were at least 13 essentials, but the rules of book

marketing prohibit greater than 9 or at most 10.) Presumably "essentials" are on the same order as habits, rules, secrets and laws.

[7] There is, coincidentally, a book by that name by Eckhart Tolle. It is a philosophical book of self-realization, and deals with the importance of "living in the Now." Although that is a different concept from what I am referring to here, it is also an insightful and valuable one, although a little too self-centered an approach to life for my tastes.

[8] For those without handy access to a teacher or book on meditation, here is a short, lay, explanation. Sit upright in a comfortable position, in a quiet room (not dark, but dimmed light is preferable). You can cross your legs, Native American style, and let your hands lie relaxed in your lap, preferably such that they form a pyramid with the thumb and forefinger of each hand touching the thumb and forefinger of the other. Close your eyes. Then mentally repeat your "mantra". The mantra is a word you do not speak out loud but repeat over and over in your mind. It can be two syllables, usually ending with an "m" for the humming quality, such as "haar-eem". The so-called "universal mantra" is "Ohm". Repeat the mantra continuously with your body in the described position and your face muscles relaxed. Try to exclude other thoughts. Within ten minutes you will find that your body and mind have entered into an altered state of deep relaxation. You might relax more if you visualize positive energy surrounding you and filling your body, and see the dark negative energy flowing out of your body. After a few more minutes, gradually come up out of it, slowly blinking your eyes open and taking some deep breaths. You will feel refreshed and ready to take on the rest of the day. Having provided you with this primer, I would suggest that, as with any life-altering behavior, you might want to consult an expert or at least get a good book on the subject.

[9] His book describes Nine Insights, clearly the right number--so much so that he had to separately write a sequel titled *The 10th Insight*—but how do insights stack up against habits, rules, secrets and laws? Since they suggest an even more innate body of knowledge, I would probably give them an edge.

[10] That business, Mobelform, is an importer and distributor of high end modern furniture. It is now run by our son-in-law, and he has done a terrific job expanding it nationally. Have a look at **www.mobelform. com.**

[11] Dr. Maxwell Maltz, a plastic surgeon who wrote *Psycho-Cybernetics* emphasized the mind as a computer which solves problems if you don't get in the way. He describes how Edison, when faced with a problem he could not solve, would take a nap and often awake with the answer.

[12] In a concession to my daughter the lawyer/psychologist, I would add a caveat that sometimes it is not healthy to ignore, deny or pretend a problem doesn't exist and keep an emotionally unsettling issue bottled up inside.

[13] He also believed he should leave the world a better place. He built the beautiful Bok Singing Tower with a nature sanctuary in Central Florida.

[14] For the latter, it is helpful to have an always thoughtful daughter like Marni to remind you.

ACKNOWLEDGMENTS

First and foremost, thanks to my parents for raising me from early childhood to always believe that I could become whatever I wanted and achieve whatever I set my sights on. It all starts with that fundamental belief system. My wife, Debbie, encouraged me to sit down and write the book and was a valuable source of ideas and continuous support. Many ideas came from many people along the way. My long time partner Gary Poliakoff was a good model for the importance of focus. My friend and former legislative aide, Alexis Castorri (herself an author on her work with athletes and others to achieve a winning attitude) for editorial suggestions. My mother, Lorraine Becker, provided line by line editing for my construction and sometimes-lacking spelling skills. One of our superstars at Becker & Poliakoff, P.A., Colleen LaPlant transcribed the interview tapes (no easy task) and typed the manuscript; and our web-master, Peter J. Nolan, for his cover design and production suggestions. Finally, I have to thank my children Marni and Ilana who, besides being great kids, are both very accomplished in their own right and are living proof that the theories in my book work well in real life.

Alan S. Becker was elected to the Florida Legislature when he was 26 and served 3 terms in the House of Representatives. That same year he founded a law firm which is now the 15th largest in Florida. He is also Honorary Consul General of the Czech Republic, representing that country in Florida, and a member of the Board of Directors of Enterprise Florida, the State's public/private economic development organization. In 2004 and 2005, he was listed by Florida Trend Magazine as one of Florida's Legal Elite, and in April,2005, South Florida CEO Magazine listed him as one of the most "powerful" people in Florida. He is Distinguished Scholar lecturer for Kaplan University, teaching college students how to achieve success after college. Alan is married with two adult daughters.

Photo:
The Alhambra Towers
Coral Gables, Florida
Developer:
The Allen Morris Company
Architecture by :
ACi Architects, Inc.
Winter Park, Florida
Photograph by Peter J. Nolan

Made in the USA